A GUIDE TO THE *Carnivores* OF CENTRAL AMERICA

CARLOS L. DE LA ROSA

CLAUDIA C. NOCKE

 University of Texas Press, Austin

A

GUIDE

TO

THE

Carnivores

OF

CENTRAL

AMERICA

Natural History,

Ecology,

and

Conservation

LIBRARY OF CONGRESS CATALOGING-IN-PUBLICATION DATA

de la Rosa, Carlos Luis.
   A guide to the carnivores of Central America : natural
history, ecology, and conservation / Carlos L. de la Rosa and
Claudia C. Nocke. — 1st ed.
      p.   cm.
   Includes bibliographical references and index.
   ISBN 0-292-71604-4 (cloth). —ISBN 0-292-71605-2 (pbk.)
   1. Carnivora—Central America.   I. Nocke, Claudia C.,
1970– .   II. Title.
QL737.C2R66   2000   99-29963
599.7′0972—dc21

CONTENTS

This book is dedicated to

CARLOS ALBERTO AND ELIZABETH MARÍA DE LA ROSA

in whose generation
lies the bulk of the
responsibility for the fate
of many of the species
described in this book.

C. DE LA R.

This book is also dedicated to

KLAUS AND ANNEMARIE NOCKE

*whose unfailing support
allowed me to dedicate the
last few years to work in
the tropics and to obtain the
experiences related here.*

C. C. N.

PREFACE

The idea of writing a guide to Central American carnivores came to us after spending many years working as researchers and conservationists in the Neotropics. Together we have spent over 13 years involved in several aspects of tropical biology, research, education, and conservation, mostly in Costa Rica and Nicaragua. In recent years, we have come to realize that the status of many species of tropical carnivores is critical. Some of the largest and most recognizable species, like the jaguar and the puma, have suffered tremendous losses to their habitats. Some of these losses have become the main reason why these species are doomed to disappear entirely from many parts of their ranges. While conservation efforts in Central America are progressing steadily throughout the region, for some of these species, the progress simply is not happening fast enough.

In this book we make some sobering observations and claims as to the future of several species of carnivores in the region. These observations are based on the present knowledge of the biological needs of the species and the immediate prospects for habitat conservation and restoration. While the situation is not terribly urgent for many species of Neotropical carnivores, for several of them the next 10 or 15 years will decide their future presence and sustainability or their disappearance from the region.

Regional efforts, such as the Central American Biological Corridor, or Paseo Pantera, are initiatives in the right direction, although the difficulties in establishing multipurpose biological corridors through an assortment of countries, economies, and cultures are numerous and complex. Conservationists tend to become involved in politics, sociology, and economics, often to the point of losing sight of what is actually best for the species and habitats they are trying to preserve. If we really want to make progress in the conservation of carnivores and their habitats, biological information about the species should be made widely available to all segments of society, not just to biologists. Politicians, economists, sociologists, and conservationists need to speak the same language. Conservation in the American tropics involves much more than choosing where parks, preserves, and biological corridors should be established. It also requires striking a balance among the specific needs of a dozen countries (some outside Central America, but with strong influences in the region) and taking into account their economic and social pressures, as well as incorporating the needs of future generations in the decision-making process.

We hope that the information in this guide, and in similar guides to come, helps bring relevant biological information to the discussion and negotiation table. Rarely is the biologist the one who decides where a conservation area will be located, nor is it the biologist who writes the laws or attempts to enforce them. This guide, then, is written with the nonbiologist in mind. Most technical terms are either explained in the text when first used or included in the glossary.

HOW TO USE THIS BOOK

This guide is divided into three parts. The introductory chapter deals with general characteristics of Central American carnivores, including their evolution, taxonomy and classification, distribution, habits, and other topics, such as vegetation types and tracking. Following the introduction, each family of Central American carnivore is presented, beginning with an introduction for each family and followed by a description of each species. We include with each description a map of species distribution where the reader can find the areas most likely to have representative populations of the species. These distribution maps differ from those commonly found in most field guides in that, in addition to showing the historic range for the species, we include the major patches of suitable habitats where the species actually can be found at present. In general terms, these patches correspond to protected areas, both private and government-supported (for example, national parks), or unprotected areas with various types of natural vegetation cover. We make no attempt to qualify these protected areas as suitable or unsuitable for specific species; as we will show in the species accounts, there is much to be learned about the habitat requirements, territories, and home ranges for most species, and this kind of information—which only long-term research can provide—is essential for managing these areas and maintaining viable populations of each species. At the end of each species description there is a conservation status summary of the species intended for quick reference. Finally, a chapter on carnivore conservation explores some of the major carnivore conservation topics and presents other pressing issues relating to the future of carnivores in Central America.

We have strived to include the latest research findings and taxonomic changes in this guide. However, carnivore taxonomy and systematics, as well as ecological research, is a very active and continuously changing field, and not all of the players are in agreement with the findings of their colleagues. We have included in the species accounts only that information which has been published in peer-reviewed scientific journals, books from recognized and reviewed publishing houses, and reports and publications from agencies involved in carnivore conservation, such as the International Union for the Conservation of Nature (IUCN), the World Wildlife Fund (WWF), and others. Our first-hand accounts of encounters with individuals of most species are intended to give insights into the lives and habits of these creatures, the places where they live, and some of the risks to which they are exposed in Central America. If these descriptions succeed in raising readers' interest in knowing a little more about these species, our goal will have been fulfilled.

ACKNOWLEDGMENTS

Many people provided inspiration and support for the work that went into this book. We would like to acknowledge Siegfried Weisel and Sabine Weber for their untiring work toward the conservation of Costa Rica's wild cats and for providing the setting for one of the authors (C. C. N.) to work with and learn from them. They also provided photo opportunities and many hours of discussions on conservation, education, and wildlife management. Their experiences and efforts have inspired us and enriched this book. We also thank Lilly and Werner Hagnauer for their fruitful discussions and for providing reference material, both live and in print, of much usefulness for this book.

We thank Len Berry from the Florida Center for Environmental Studies (CES) of Florida Atlantic University and Ken Cummins and Pat Gostel from the South Florida Water Management District (SFWMD) for supporting the authors during the writing of the final manuscript.

We would also like to acknowledge the following individuals and organizations for providing information, support, or assistance during the field activities that are related in the book: the Costa Rican Wildlife Department and the National Park Service (now parts of the Ministry of the Environment and Energy, or MINAE), particularly Alexandra Sáenz, Juan Rodríguez, Sigifredo Marín, and the staff of the Santa Rosa, Guanacaste, Palo Verde, Tenorio, and other national parks; the Organization of American States (OAS) in their Sustainable Development of the San Juan River Watershed Project, Nicaragua and Costa Rica, particularly Juan José Castro, Alekcey Chuprine, Rigoberto Argüello, Mario Rodríguez, Rossy Araya, and the rest of the staff and consultants that worked on the project; the staff and members of the Heliconia Biological Field Station, especially Marvin Jiménez and his family, for the many hours spent in the field learning about the plants and animals they are in charge of protecting, and for showing what real conservationists can do; Pablo Riba and Lucía de la Osa for sharing their experiences in Osa Península; Tadeu Gomes de Oliveira for sharing his book and his knowledge of Neotropical cats; Elías Chávez, Marco Fischer, Geraldine Kleinsasser, Stine Christiansen, Walter Odio, and all the other volunteers and supporters of PROFELIS; Daniel Janzen and Winnie Hallwachs for providing the setting and inspiration, and for supporting one of the authors (C. de la R.) in his projects and activities in Central America, particularly in Costa Rica; the U.S. Agency for International Development (USAID), especially Arturo Villalobos and the staff of AGRIDEC, particularly Bernardo Pestano, Federico Poey, Nancy Fong, and George Primov, for their support during C. de la R.'s work in northern Costa Rica; Mario Boza for sharing his ideas and enthusiasm for the Meso-American Biological Corridor; Sorrell Downer and the staff of Green Arrow for their efforts in supporting volunteers for our Costa Rican projects; and Antonio Ruiz and the staff of the Fundación del Río in Nicaragua for hosting the authors every time we traveled to that wonderful country.

Finally, C. de la R. would like to acknowledge the contributions of Mary Patricia de la Rosa and Charlie and Lizzy de la Rosa for sharing and participating in some of the most exciting years of his life living and working on the slopes of the Orosí Volcano in Costa Rica. We would like to thank Lizzy de la Rosa for the skull illustrations.

The staff of the University of Texas Press proved to be instrumental in making this book more readable, enjoyable, and organized. Their contributions, as well as those from two anonymous reviewers, were substantial. We'd like to acknowledge especially Shannon Davies, Sheri Englund, Mandy Woods, Allison Faust, Teresa Wingfield, and Nancy Bryan, as well as the rest of the staff and reviewers associated with the press.

A GUIDE TO THE *Carnivores* OF CENTRAL AMERICA

The Order Carnivora

in Central America

INTRODUCTION TO THE ORDER CARNIVORA

If there is a group of mammals that has always fascinated humans, it is the carnivores. There is evidence of carnivore interactions (friendly and unfriendly) with humans from the earliest days of recorded history. Lions, tigers, and other carnivores appear prominently in Greek mythology (Gittelman, 1989), on the walls of Egyptian tombs, and in many biblical references. Ancient and yet understudied petroglyphs near the Orosí volcano in northern Costa Rica depict spotted cats and other animals. Today, our most common pets, the domestic dog and cat, are descendants of wild carnivores. When we go to the zoo, the crowds usually gather at the exhibits of the lions, tigers, wolves, otters, and bears—all carnivores. We wear (or used to wear) their pelts, both in primitive and in modern societies.

Carnivores have inspired fear and respect in every continent in the world where they are found. Hunters pursue carnivore trophies with more zeal than any other prey, and many wildlife management programs in the Americas, India, and Africa focus on carnivores. For farmers in many parts of the world, carnivores are foes competing for resources, killing cattle, sheep, chickens, and other domestic animals, even though much of the fear and the blame carnivores get is unfounded. Even in areas where damage done by carnivores is very hard to document, the sighting of a coyote, an ocelot, or a jaguar immediately brings out the guns. Someone lost in one of the remaining jungles of Central America probably fears an encounter with a jaguar (an almost impossible occurrence, given their declining populations and their shyness around humans) with the same intensity as he or she fears poisonous snakes, a more realistic threat.

On the other hand, our friendly relationship—even collaboration—with carnivores is also long and well documented (Ewer, 1973). Besides adopting several species as pets, humans have used carnivores, such as cheetahs, as hunting companions, depending on their speed and sense of smell to help locate game. Cheetahs, caracals, and civets have been trained to help people hunt in Africa, and otters have been used in China to drive fish under nets. Given their relatively high intelligence, many species also have been tamed and trained to entertain. Bears, lions, and tigers are staples in circus spectacles, and most other species have been kept as pets at one time or another, even skunks. It is their close association with humans, as well as their intelligence, that have made the carnivores an important part of human activities for millennia.

While our fascination with carnivores is likely to continue, our knowledge of their biology, their habits, and their habitats lags far behind. In Central America, home to 24 species of carnivores, the general population's knowledge about this group is particularly shallow. People seldom realize that our daily companions (dogs and cats) mirror behaviors and habits of their wilder relatives. Scientists have been increasingly concerned over the years about the general population's ignorance (especially in rural areas) of even the most basic aspects of carnivore biology and behavior. For instance, in the authors' workshops with educators and students in rural Costa Rica, our comparisons of domestic cats and dogs with jaguars, ocelots, and pumas always brought laughs of incredulity. Statements such as "a jaguar or a puma is just like a little house cat, except a lot bigger" were received with smiles. Only when we went into details, comparing skull specimens, looking at films and photographs, and identifying all those behaviors also common to our house cats (grooming, stalking, chewing, claw sharpening, etc.), did people begin to realize that these fierce wild predators, often considered enemies of the farmer and the rancher, are simply following their natural instincts shared by other members of their family. And, more importantly—and one of the points of this book—if we observe and study the domestic relatives of carnivores, we can begin to learn how to coexist and adapt our ranching or farming routines (under which we include hunting) to avoid conflict.

CARNIVORE EVOLUTION: CENTRAL AMERICA AND THE GREAT NORTH—SOUTH MIGRATIONS

When did the first carnivores evolve? It is believed that they evolved from animals similar to insectivores about 55 million years ago, during the Paleocene. The first carnivores looked very much like weasels and have been classified into two families, now extinct: the Miacidae and the Viverridae. During the Paleocene other meat-eating mammals existed, particularly the Creodonta, which also became extinct. Interestingly, the Creodonta shared with carnivores the carnassial, or meat-shearing, teeth which have evolved independently several times among mammals.

Members of the Canidae (dogs), Felidae (cats), Mustelidae (weasels), and Viverridae (mongooses) families had evolved by the early Oligocene, followed by the Ursidae (bears) in the late Oligocene or early Miocene. The figure below illustrates the approximate times that the different modern families of carnivores separated from the mother stocks.

The radiation and rapid speciation of carnivores paralleled the evolution and appearance of many prey species, which in turn appeared in response to the proliferation of plant types available as food. The Pliocene and the Pleistocene also saw the appearance and later disappearance of giant species in many mammalian families. Among the carnivores, the quite formidable

Family tree for the Order Carnivora.

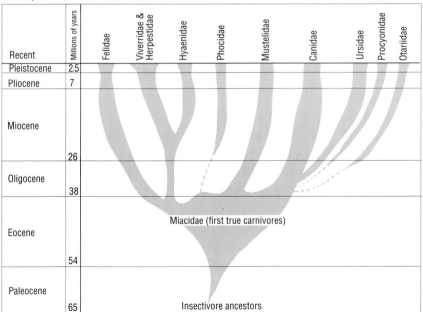

saber-toothed cats (for example, the genera *Smilodon* and *Megantereon*, contemporary with early humans) are an impressive example of this pattern. While they were no larger than a modern tiger, their 23-cm canines probably allowed them to kill thick-skinned prey such as giant sloths, mastodons, and elephants. They became extinct about 12,000 years ago. In modern times, most carnivore families are composed of small species with less impressive weapons.

Central America is part of the Neotropical Region, which comprises the lands between Mexico and Patagonia. It includes the isthmus between North and South America and a series of islands that form an arch loosely connecting Florida with the northern part of South America (Venezuela). There is a great diversity of habitats in the Neotropics, and a great number of carnivores as well.

This book is concerned with the region that extends from Guatemala, at the southern border of Mexico, to Panama, where it joins Colombia and the rest of South America. This narrow strip of land has been for millions of years a series of bridges, connecting and disconnecting the two great land masses of North and South America. The connections have appeared several times, the latest during the late Miocene and the Pliocene, and each time migrations and exchanges of flora and fauna have occurred. During the late Eocene, the land bridge between Nicaragua, Costa Rica, and Panama was broken, allowing the mixture of the waters from the Atlantic and the Pacific oceans. The connection reappeared as a series of violently active volcanoes, allowing in time the floras and faunas of South America, Central America, and the Caribbean islands to mix. Later, during the Pliocene and Recent times, the connection between Central America and Mexico (at the Tehuantepec Straight) closed, allowing the full exchange between North and South America.

Several orders of mammals, including primates and marsupials, crossed this bridge between the Cretaceous and the Eocene, going mostly from north to south. During the Pliocene-Pleistocene, the bridge was crossed by the carnivores, the Proboscidea (relatives of modern elephants), Artiodactyla (relatives of pigs, peccaries, camels, and deer, among others), and Perissodactyla (relatives of horses and tapirs). Thus this periodically occurring bridge has given Central America a richness in species of plants and animals. This book will identify in the species descriptions a number of species that also live in northern Temperate regions.

Because Central America is a biologically rich region, there are an abundance of habitats and ecosystems where carnivores thrive. However, there has been extensive deforestation and conversion of natural habitats to pas-

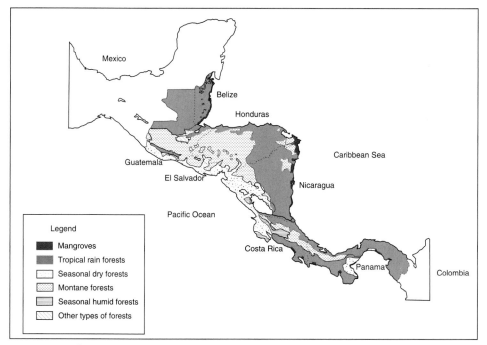

1. *Central American vegetation types.*

tures and agriculture in the last 200 years, and much of the original forested areas have all but disappeared.

Map 1 shows the main vegetation types that are found in Central America. However, not all of these areas are actually covered with forest. Map 2 shows the remaining forested areas in Central America.

As illustrated in Map 2, the natural vegetation connection has been broken in several places, leaving a series of patches or islands of natural habitats along the isthmus. Some of these patches are national parks or other protected areas, but many are not under any protection plan and are at risk of disappearing in the next decade or two.

Many carnivore species have adapted to living in disturbed areas (some of them actually have thrived and prospered following deforestation), and thus can be found in areas where the natural vegetation has disappeared or has been replaced by other types of land use. The coyote, for example, originally adapted to live in savannas and areas with sparse vegetation, has lately extended its range into Central America, in part following the man-made changes in land-use patterns. While 100 years ago coyotes were hardly seen in Central America, they are now a common feature in most of the region, feeding on road kills, in garbage dumps, and on domestic stock.

We can safely say that the faunal exchanges that have occurred throughout the history of Central America continue today, aided both by natural and

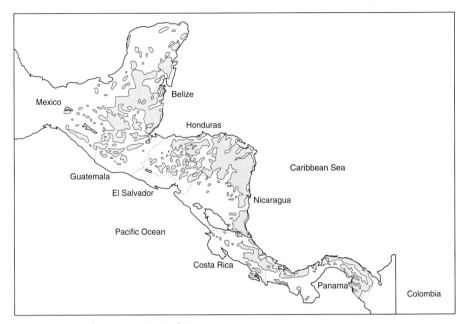

2. *Remaining forests in Central America.*

man-made forces. The current distribution patterns we see in the species treated in this book are likely to continue changing rapidly, as more natural habitats are destroyed or modified irreversibly. On the other hand, reforestation and habitat rehabilitation projects, such as the Guanacaste Conservation Area in northern Costa Rica and the Central American Biological Corridor project or Paseo Pantera, will bring some species back to parts of their former ranges.

VEGETATION TYPES IN CENTRAL AMERICA

Every species, whether it is a carnivore or a herbivore, a bird or an insect, has a preferred type of habitat in which it thrives (what biologists call adapted to that particular habitat). Many species can survive in other habitats, but in general terms, there is a place where a species optimally balances food intake and energy spent in hunting or foraging, reproducing, and acquiring and maintaining shelter. Often the habitat preferences of a species have to do with its requirements for surviving and thriving (the amount of food it needs, for example) and the availability of unbroken areas of habitat that provide it with all its needs.

Some species are very particular about their habitat requirements (biologists call them specialized), while others are more generalist and adaptable to a variety of habitats. There are advantages and disadvantages to being either a habitat specialist or a generalist; in the present state of the remaining natural habitats in Central America, the generalists have an advantage in that they have more choices of where to live. Still, Central America is rich in available types of habitats for carnivores, and this is best reflected in the major vegetation types found throughout. There are many more habitat types than the ones described (for example, the areas where one vegetation type meets another, or ecotones) which create whole gradations of habitat characteristics (temperature, rainfall, species composition, etc.), but the major types are clearly distinguishable and illustrative of the richness of the region. One only would have to drive a few hours in Costa Rica to be able to visit several of these vegetation types, which would take days, if not weeks, to do in North or South America. What follows is a description of the major vegetation types found in Central America.

TROPICAL RAIN FOREST

This is the most extensive of all vegetation forms, present mainly in the Caribbean coastal plain to about 900 meters elevation. This forest type contains a large number of species, including many woody plants of economic importance, such as fig trees (*Ficus*), chicle trees (*Manilkara*), and many others. Characteristic of these forests are tree ferns, lianas, and vines, and a variety of epiphytes, such as orchids and bromeliads. Mangrove forests, palms, and salt-tolerant plants are found along rivers and through swamps and coastal areas.

SEASONAL DRY FOREST

This is seasonally deciduous forest to evergreen woodlands, covering at one time most of the Pacific lowlands and slopes to about 1,000 meters in elevation. Today, less than 2% of the original 550,000 square kilometers of undisturbed forest remains, most of it outside protected areas (Janzen, 1986). In this type of forest, the deciduous trees lose their leaves (in complex species-specific patterns) through the dry season, which is also the flowering time for many of these trees. Human conversion of most of these forests, due to their rich soils, has created so-called "savannas," or grasslands, and agricultural lands. Gallery forests (forests along streams and rivers) tend to be taller than the surrounding forests and less deciduous because of their proximity to water; however, they are not a distinct category. Some typical native dry forest trees are the boxwood tree (*Hura*), the ear tree (*Enterolobium cyclocarpum*), *Ceiba*, *Cassia grandis*, *Bombax*, and *Ficus*, all of which can grow tall with large spreading crowns. Smaller trees like *Hymenaea* (stinking toe), *Coccoloba* (relative of the sea grape), *Cochlospermum*, *Guazuma* (Guácimo), *Bursera simaruba* (naked Indian), and others, as well as palms such as *Acrocomia,* are also typical. In Belize, a coniferous forest (*Pinus caribaea*) and a broadleaf deciduous open woodland occurs.

XEROPHYTIC VEGETATION AREAS
Semi-arid conditions, coupled with human intervention, have created areas where thorn-brush, cactus, and scrubby trees abound. These occur in some highlands of Guatemala, Honduras, and El Salvador. Typical examples are the middle portion of the Rio Negro (Guatemala) and the upper Aguán Valley (Honduras).

MONTANE FORESTS
At between 1,000 and 1,500 meters in elevation, temperate species begin to replace tropical ones as elevation increases. Oaks (*Quercus*) and epiphytes are common at these elevations. Location with reference to slopes (Pacific or Caribbean side of the mountains) and trade winds principally define the boundaries of these areas. Cloud forests develop at elevations above 1,200 meters where high humidity levels, caused by an almost constant cloud cover and frequent precipitation, allow the development of dense broadleaf forests covered with epiphytes. Many of these forests, together with dry forests, have been converted first to agricultural land and later to grazing land. These occur in western Panama, Costa Rica, and parts of Guatemala and Honduras.

ALPINE VEGETATION AREAS
In Guatemala, these mountain forests are almost boreal, composed of coniferous trees. Montane forests are replaced at elevations above 3,000 meters in southeastern Costa Rica and western Panama by grasses, mosses, and shrubs in a plant community known as paramo.

CARNIVORE FAMILIES AND THEIR PHYLOGENETIC RELATIONSHIPS

TAXONOMY AND CLASSIFICATION
The name Carnivora is derived from the Latin words *carnis*, which means "flesh," and *vorare*, which means "to eat." Carnivora, thus, means "meat eaters." There are eleven families of carnivores, which include over 90 genera and over 230 species distributed throughout the world. Listing first the families included in this book, these families are (Wozencraft, 1995):

Felidae (cats)
Procyonidae (raccoons and coatis)
Mustelidae (skunks, weasels, badgers, grisons, and otters)
Canidae (dogs, wolves, jackals, coyotes, and foxes)
Herpestidae (mongooses)
Hyaenidae (hyenas)
Odobenidae (walruses)
Otariidae (eared seals)
Phocidae (earless seals)
Ursidae (bears)
Viverridae (civets)

The carnivores are represented in Central America by 24 species (and a variable number of subspecies, depending on which reference one refers to), making it a diverse and important group of Neotropical mammals. Of the eleven families that comprise the order, four are represented in Central America: the wild cats (Felidae), the raccoon and its relatives *(Procyonidae)*, the weasel family (Mustelidae), and the wild dogs (Canidae). The order also includes one other family in the Americas, the bears (Ursidae). These occur in North and South America but not in Central America. Some biologists consider ringtails a separate family (Bassariscidae), although here we include them in the Procyonidae.

CARNIVORE NATURAL HISTORY

Natural history, by definition, is the study of organisms, their habits, behaviors, habitats, and related natural phenomena. It examines what a species is and what makes it different (or similar) to other species; it explores the interrelationships between predator and prey and the habitats that support them; and it explains the origin and function of physical structures, as well as some of the evolutionary forces that might have influenced the appearance or disappearance of such structures and adaptations. Thus, natural history looks at the many details of the life of plants and animals; at its most basic level, it reflects our overall knowledge of a given species. This intimate knowledge ultimately will allow humans to manage and conserve for perpetuity animal and plant species and their associated habitats. To the authors, natural history is the most important area of science relating to the conservation and survival of carnivores and of other organisms. However, as we hope is obvious in this book, we need to invest more effort in basic natural history studies to stem the tide of extinction and the decline of many important populations of plants and animals.

What distinguishes a carnivore from other mammals? Carnivores are a large and ubiquitous family of mammals; they are found in every continent except Antarctica and a few oceanic islands, although they have been introduced in these places as pets, for sport, and for rodent control, usually causing more damage than good in most cases. They range in size from the gigantic Alaskan brown bears or grizzlies (*Ursus arctos*), which can weigh up to 770 kg, and the polar bears (*Ursus maritimus*), weighing up to 650 kg, to the least weasel (*Mustela nivalis*), which only attains an adult weight of up to 60 g. As we stated above, the name *carnivore* literally means "meat eater," although some species rarely stray from vegetarian meals. With such great ranges in size, distribution, body function, and diet, what traits are shared by carnivores that justify placing them in the same order?

Perhaps the only trait that unites carnivores, past and present, into one coherent evolutionary group is the presence of a modified variation of the carnassial teeth (the first lower molar and the fourth upper premolar), which are modified to act as shearing tools for cutting flesh. The carnassial teeth, if followed through the evolutionary tree of carnivores, represent the trademark of the carnivore species, even for those that do not have them presently, such as the panda and other omnivore species whose carnassial teeth have flattened to suit their nonmeat diets.

Also characteristic of carnivores is the specialized hinging of the lower jaw driven by powerful muscles, which allows it to move vertically but not horizontally; carnivores generally swallow their meat in chunks, without chewing it. They have a simple stomach and a relatively short intestine. Other shared characteristics of all carnivores are: the fusion of a number of bones from the wrists, irrespective of the mode of walking (plantigrade or digitigrade); the reduction of the collar bone or clavicle; the generally slender and agile body which is well adapted to the pursuit of prey; and the presence of powerful sets of jaw muscles well adapted to the pressure needed for killing and dismembering prey. Collectively, with some exceptions, these characteristics separate carnivores from all other groups of mammals.

FOOD HABITS

While presenting several specializations for meat eating, most carnivores also include plants in their diets, among them fruits, seeds, and grasses. The felids are perhaps the most carnivorous of all, while the canids and the procyonids exploit a wide variety of food items, making them more like omnivores. Most Central American species, perhaps with the exception of the river otter (*Lontra longicaudis*) and the puma (*Puma concolor*), are heavy fruit eaters. Coyote feces, for example, are often full of seeds such as *Ficus* spp. (wild figs), *Manilkara zapota* (chicle tree), *Genipa americana*, *Byrsonima crassifolia* (shoemaker's tree), and other species. This is evidence of their varied eating habits and the long distances traveled in their search for food. We have encountered coyote scats with typical forest fruits and seeds miles away from the nearest forest. We have also observed coyotes gorging themselves on the ripe—and mildly alcoholic—fruits of *Byrsonima crassifolia*, lapping up the fruits off the ground, swallowing them whole, and then taking long naps (perhaps due to a little intoxication?) at the base of these trees. Some coyotes even showed a preference for certain individual trees that upon testing were found to produce sweeter fruits than others nearby. Many of these fruits pass whole through their digestive tracts and can be recognized easily in their scats. Similarly, feces of the tayra (*Eira barbara*), the raccoon (*Procyon lotor*), and the coati (*Nasua narica*) almost always have seeds in them.

Most Central American carnivores disperse many of these seeds after they pass intact through their relatively simple digestive tracts. Whether these animals are "good" or "bad" seed dispersers depends on the biology of the plant (Janzen, 1983). High frugivory, or fruit-eating, among carnivores is also common in temperate regions. There is an abundance of fruits and seeds in the scats of bears, raccoons, foxes, and coyotes from North America, which opportunistically exploit this food resource during fruiting season. However, there are perhaps more opportunities to be frugivorous in the tropics than in temperate regions, as many plant species fruit at different times of the year. A large number of these fruits are fleshy, loaded with sugars, vitamins, proteins, and fats, and packaged in "containers" suitable to a wide range of animals.

However, not all carnivores restrict their diets to naturally occurring foods. Bears are notorious "garbage pickers" in North America, and even polar bears visit garbage dumps regularly. In Central America, coyotes dig through garbage dumps and pits and are fond of stealing edible items from porches and outside laundry rooms. Raccoons, because of their intelligence and great manual dexterity, have learned to open trash cans, garbage bags, and even cars and cellar windows to gain access to food and scraps. Skunks are easily habituated to human presence and can be enticed to come to feeding places near houses (or even inside houses).

During a trip to Playa Naranjo in Santa Rosa National Park in northern

Costa Rica, three raccoons broke through a small window of our jeep and enjoyed a week's worth of food supplies. They picked one of the side window locks and forced their way through the small opening. We also observed in Santa Rosa National Park several skunks who had the run of one of the houses where the owners fed them kitchen scraps. Some would walk through the front door, go to the kitchen, check the garbage pails for scraps, and walk out the door again, unbothered by our presence and our photo flashes.

REPRODUCTION

Carnivores have a wide range of reproductive strategies. Common to most carnivores (hyenas being the exception) is the presence of the baculum or penis bone (also known as *os penis*), a slender bone located inside the penis. The function of the bone is to prolong copulation, particularly in those species where ovulation is induced by copulation. The shape of the baculum is unique for each species and can be used for positive identification of skeletal remains.

Any owner of a dog of reproductive age has witnessed the phenomenon of the "copulation lock," or copulatory tie. During copulation, the tip of the penis engorges and enlarges substantially from its original size. The combination of the engorged glans, the baculum, and the dogs' back-to-back orientation actually locks the male and female in the copulatory position, anywhere from a few minutes to up to an hour or more. The adaptive advantage of this mechanism is not well understood, but it is believed to cement the pair bond between the male and female. This behavior occurs only in canids.

It is not difficult to imagine the carnivore's sense of smell playing an important role in functions other than hunting. Territories are defined by marks offering visual as well as olfactory warnings to would-be trespassers. Carnivores use more than urine and feces to scent-mark places in their territories. Many species possess specialized glands in different parts of their bodies which they use to scent-mark, and these glands are inspected and smelled by members of the other sex. Canids and felids, for example, smell each other's nether parts when meeting, clearly picking up scents and clues that are beyond our present state of knowledge. The combination of visual, auditory, and olfactory signs can easily be imagined as a complex language, useful in inter- and intra-specific interactions.

Little is known about the reproductive habits of many Central American carnivores. While for some species information is available, it usually refers to populations in temperate or subtropical areas, where the species might be picking up different environmental clues to time their reproductive cycles for increased success. Northern temperate winters shape many traits of species that extend their ranges into these regions. It is well known, for example, that the coat of the long-tailed weasel (*Mustela frenata*) changes to an almost all-white color during the northern winters, while the white coloration, a clear adaptation for snow-covered country, does not appear in the tropical populations. Similarly, the timing of the reproductive cycles in temperate regions responds to the changes in temperature, food availability, and other environmental changes. These environmental clues are less well understood in tropical regions.

ABUNDANCE AND DISTRIBUTION

As mentioned above, land-dwelling carnivores are found around the world, with the exception of some islands and Antarctica. Australia's only carnivore is the dingo, although it was probably introduced to the continent by the aborigines. Some other species of carnivores presently found in Australia, such as the red fox (*Vulpes vulpes*), have been recent introductions.

In Central America, carnivores inhabit just about every habitat available, from the cloud forests and paramos, to the lowland rain forests, beaches, and rivers. Being at the top of the food pyramid, their numbers are normally lower than many other mammals. However, habitat loss and other human pressures have contributed to make carnivores relatively rare or endangered throughout much of their former ranges. Some species, such as the coyote, coati, raccoon, and the skunks, have adapted relatively well to human presence, often moving into human settlements and making a living from the scraps of civilization.

The distribution and habitats of many species of Central American carnivores are poorly understood. For some species there is hardly any data; carnivore research is urgently needed. In this book, we have extrapolated some information available for similar (congeneric) species. Unfortunately, there are no reliable estimates at this time of the number of carnivores in Central America.

TRACKS, TRAILS, AND SIGNS

While the fine art of animal tracking is beyond the scope of this book, there are a few pointers that would make more enjoyable the observation and study of Central American carnivores for the nonscientist. Many species are rare and very hard to see. In all the years trekking through some very wild and remote areas of Costa Rica and Nicaragua, the authors have failed to encounter a wild jaguar face to face. However, tracks and signs of their presence have been readily available. Some of these signs were fresh enough to make us look over our shoulders and into the surrounding vegetation with a healthy dose of concern. Learning to recognize some of these signs can provide interesting and rewarding experiences in the field.

The best way to track an animal is through knowledge of the animal's habits. Often in the tropics one finds one track, seemingly isolated on the side of a trail, barely perceptible in the soft cushion of leaves and mud. While we seldom follow tracks in the forest, a few tracks can tell us much about the animal that left them. Carnivore tracks are not difficult to learn, and we provide in the text some details on how to recognize the most common species. However, carnivores leave many other signs in a given area, if we know where to look.

Many species of canids, cats, and mustelids like to follow human trails and roads, perhaps for the same reason we use them: it is easier to travel on them than through the vegetation. We have encountered coyotes, skunks, pumas, tayras, and other species on trails (and even on some major roads, pavement and all), and have seen tracks of jaguars and other more elusive species on forest trails and near human dwellings. The often muddy conditions of these roads and paths near rural habitations are excellent for preserving tracks.

In most cases, nonexperts can identify tracks to family or genera (seldom to species, except in the case of very unique species). To properly identify species one needs skills, tools, and reference materials beyond the reach of most part-time naturalists. However, the track of a large cat such as a jaguar or a puma is impressive and hard to misidentify. Tracks are usually part of a trail, that is, a set of tracks that the animal leaves while walking or running; these trails form unique patterns associated with particular species or genera. In forested areas, trail patterns are often very difficult to observe, and even more difficult to interpret. Tracks and trail patterns vary with the age of the animal, as well as with its behavior (walking, trotting, running, stalking, etc.). Learning to recognize all of these patterns requires patience, training, and many hours in the field.

One can observe and learn the basic tracks left by many species by visiting zoos or by observing captive animals. Also, when traveling through wild areas, local guides are often familiar with the tracks left by the most common species.

Scats are often quite unique among carnivores, and one can distinguish and identify with relative ease the scats of felids, canids, and other groups. A word of caution is necessary here. Most—if not all—wild carnivores carry parasites in their intestines; the eggs, larvae, or adults are left in the scats and can be harmful to humans. Raccoons, for example, carry parasites whose microscopic eggs can infest humans if inhaled. Leptospirosis, a very dangerous and widespread bacteria, can be transmitted to humans through contact with the urine of wild mammals. Never touch an animal scat with your bare hands, not even an obviously old and dry scat. You may want to use the scat to investigate what the animal ate, since they often pass intact many bones, fur, bird feathers and beaks, and other "goodies." If you care to do such studies, do so with sticks and while wearing gloves. Also, try to keep your face away from dry scats, since they often carry fungal spores or parasite eggs that can be inhaled accidentally.

While examining scats, look for the remains of prey (bones, feathers, claws, beaks, and fur), as well as remains of crustaceans (common in raccoons and in some felids, and very abundant in otters), fish scales, insect parts, seeds, undigested fruits, and other plant parts. Near human habitations, you may find pieces of plastic, paper, and leather. Finding a "latrine" or area where individuals of several species defecate on a regular basis can offer a wealth of information about the feeding habits of a species, if you can overcome what may be a natural squeamishness about digging through feces. As a small consolation, we offer the fact that most wild animal scats are relatively odorless or have only a mild smell, which is often fruity, musky, or "gamy." Domestic animals (cats and dogs in particular) have potent and often offending feces mainly because of the artificial food we provide to them. It is logical, then, that wild canids who rummage through garbage dumps or those kept in captivity often develop scat smells that resemble those of domestic dogs.

While in the forest, look for scrape areas, claw marks on trees, and places where prey remains have been buried. Wild cats often bury their leftovers with surrounding litter; the size of the cleared forest floor around the burial mound can be an indication of the animal that made it. The site of remains buried by a large wild cat (jaguar or puma) is unmistakable and truly impressive. If it is fresh, look for other signs of the animal (scent, tracks, or depositions), for it seldom strays too far from the place of its recent unfinished meal. It might actually hide nearby and observe your rummaging of its dinner!

We often use our sense of smell when walking on wild trails. While human sense of smell is no match for that of other animals, it can be useful if properly attuned to wildlife scents. A good place to practice identifying the scents of different species is the local zoo or animal rescue shelter. Cat urine, deposited ritualistically in specific places around enclosures or cages, is very pungent and unique. Note that it is also corrosive and stains clothes. If near the cage or enclosure of a wild cat, look for places where it urinates (or observe the animal for a while until it sprays). By positioning oneself in the path of the wind, one can pick up the odor and learn to recognize it in the field. The scent of a skunk is easily recognized by anyone who travels country roads in the Americas; the identification of the odor of urine and other scents from other species can also be learned.

Dens and hiding places can often be identified by following tracks or trails that lead to them. Be careful if the den seems recently inhabited or in use. A nursing female, even of a small species, can become a formidable adversary if she perceives a threat to her litter. If you find young of any species, do not handle them or move them at all. They are not lost or abandoned, and the mother is probably nearby. You increase the risk of danger to the young ones and to yourself by handling or disturbing them.

Tracking and observing signs left by wildlife is a rewarding and often forgotten art. It was part of the survival skills of our ancestors, and it can become a useful tool in research and conservation. Much information about the habits and habitats used by a species can be gathered from the study of animal tracks and signs, and this increased knowledge and better data will improve our understanding of the needs of these species.

The Wild Cats

Family
FELIDAE

The Wild Cats

Cats are the ultimate hunting machines, adapted to stalking, chasing, grabbing, and rapidly killing live prey with efficiency, raw power, and speed.
Among the 36 or so species of wild cats in the world, there are variations on
these skills, where one species excels at speed (such as the cheetah), others at
stalking (such as the jaguar or the leopard), and others at fishing (such as the
Asian fishing cat). One is even a plant-loving cat (the flat-headed cat), which
also feeds on, in addition to regular meat, fruits and roots such as sweet
potatoes.

Morphologically, most cats share adaptations that bear the "hunter" signature prominently. They have the least number of teeth of the terrestrial
carnivores (only some weasels come close to having as few teeth), but these
are highly specialized for meat processing, particularly the carnassial teeth.
Their incisors are small and undifferentiated, especially when compared to
the large and pointed canines. Cats have lost most premolars, so usually
there is a space between the canines and the molars (with the exception of
the cheetah, which is in more ways than one an unusual cat). The carnassials
are strong and well-developed. Because they are clearly and uniquely adapted
to cutting meat, these teeth have no grinding or chewing surfaces; the mas-

sive musculature necessary to make them work allows little lateral movement. Thus cats swallow pieces of meat whole, without chewing, and depend on their strong digestive enzymes to break down the meal. Finally, cats
have a rough, rasplike surface on their tongues, with which they can dis-
lodge skin from flesh or flesh from bones. Add to this arsenal of weapons a
set of retractable claws (except in the cheetah), kept incredibly sharp by a series of behaviors readily observed in the house cat, and you have a superbly
adapted carnivore.

Within the cat family, there is an incredible amount of variation in some
of their traits, but the overall pattern and familial characteristics are there.
Some species are completely terrestrial (lion), while others like the water
(jaguar, fishing cat), or take to the trees (margay). Occupied habitats range
from sea level, through deserts, scrub lands, and rain forests, to cloud forests
and paramos. There are jungle cats, pampas cats, grassland cats, sand cats,
and even mountain and snow cats.

In general, sight and smell are the most developed senses in felids. Their
sensitive whiskers allow them to move through small spaces in the dark
avoiding obstructions. While cats are no match for canids regarding their
sense of smell, they do rely on it to locate and approach potential prey. However, most cats (with the exception of cheetahs and, perhaps, jaguars) are
mostly nocturnal, and, hunting at night, they benefit from their highly developed eyes. Most cats stalk their prey as far as they can and then rush it,
accomplishing the kill with a choking bite to the neck.

One unique characteristic of cats is their range of vocalizations, from con-
tented purring to the snarling, hissing, spitting, and even roaring of larger
cats, all expressed according to the occasion and prevailing mood. Cats are
quieter than dogs, but they can be extremely vocal given the right circumstances. The "cough" of a jaguar in the middle of a forest on a dark Central
American night can be hair-raising. On the other hand, the purring cat
seems to involve its whole body in this pleasurable state. It is quite impressive to hear a puma purr. Mating and fighting cats are capable of a wide
range of sounds also, from low, threatening growls to ear-piercing, "bloody-
murder" screams.

Cats mark territories in several ways. Both males and females spray urine
on trees, bushes, and other points along their territories, but males, who
generally hold larger territories, spray more. Cats also use "scratching
posts," believed to serve the dual function of a territory marker and a place
to sharpen claws. Any domestic cat owner learns quickly that scratching
posts are not only essential, but that each cat has its specific requirements
for this part of its environment. Why a couch's arm or a chair's leg would be

so much more attractive than a specially purchased carpet-covered post is still a mystery to some of us. Cats also show other ritualized behaviors. These include patterns of behavior that are repeated across species and that seem innate rather than learned. For example, scratching and burying feces and urine is innate, and even little kittens raised by humans begin to do these things without prodding. Stalking and pouncing are behaviors common to kittens at play and mimic adult hunting behaviors.

In Central America, there are six species of Felidae. Two are large cats (the jaguar and the puma); three are spotted cats (the ocelot, the margay, and the tiger cat, in order of diminishing size); and the unusual jaguarundi, which comes in two color morphs, cinnamon and bluish/gray or black. Most of them are given some protection status in Central America, but the combination of habitat loss, pet trade, the market for pelts, and unfounded fears in humans have combined to doom most of the species throughout the region. Some countries, such as El Salvador, have no suitable habitat left for the big cats, while Guatemala, Honduras, and Costa Rica are close to losing the battle of maintaining viable populations of the big species. It is our belief that the combination of direct and indirect threats, rather than a single issue, endanger these species. Indirect threats, such as human overcrowding in small protected areas, overhunting of prey species, lack of coherent environmental education programs, and ineffective legislation add their combined weight to the survival pressures on these species.

Cats, like other carnivores, play important roles in the balance of tropical ecosystems. As top predators, they help maintain healthy prey populations. The continued and traditional exploitation of cats for their pelts, as well as for the pet trade, have all but eliminated these fierce predators from most of their range. All species in Central America are under various degrees of protection, at least on paper. However, this protection will be in vain if we do not learn to respect and appreciate the role these species play in the balance of nature.

JAGUAR

(Panthera onca)

It was about 11 P.M. on a moonless night in Guanacaste, northern Costa Rica. In the enveloping darkness, Manuel and Javier, caretakers of the Maritza Biological Field Station in Guanacaste National Park, returned on horseback from a trip to the nearest town some 10 miles away. Loaded with supplies and tired of the long ride, they allowed their horses to pick their

Portrait of male jaguar.

footing on the narrow trail that led to the station through the thick forests that blanketed the sides of the Cacao and Orosí volcanoes. Their flashlights were tucked away in their saddle bags. They trusted their mounts to follow the familiar path. A light rain filtered through the canopy and drenched the exposed soil, creating a sticky mud that made sucking noises at every step of the horses. There was near total darkness. Horses are known to have excellent sense of smell, and both horses kept their noses down, perhaps following their own scent which was left there on their previous passing.

Suddenly, Javier's horse, who was leading, stopped and snorted nervously.

His ears pricked forward toward the blackness ahead. Manuel, some 50 yards behind, spurred his own horse to keep it going, finding it difficult to make it obey his orders. When it reached Javier's, both horses refused to continue, snorting and trying to turn back on the trail.

"I bet there's a snake on the trail," Javier said, reaching back to his saddle bag for the flashlight. Manuel followed suit. They both turned on their lights and the bright beams probed the darkness, illuminating the trail in front of them. They could see nothing. The horses still refused to go on, requiring the riders to keep tight reins lest they lose control of their mounts. A heavy feeling of foreboding began to fill the men's hearts. With their lights they scanned the trail and the forest directly ahead of them, searching for the cause of the horses' near-panicky behavior.

"Oh my God!" Javier whispered between clenched teeth. Manuel's light beam joined Javier's. Reflecting some 50 yards ahead on the trail were the two incandescent coals of the eyes of an enormous jaguar, framed by a round face about the size of a soccer ball. It was lying in the middle of the trail, motionless, attention fully concentrated on the intruders to its territory. Time seemed to stop. For several interminable minutes the jaguar and the men awaited one or the other's next move . . .

Jaguars are not commonly seen in the wild. Recently, in Costa Rica's Santa Rosa National Park, there have been several daytime sightings of jaguars, including a female with a cub that boldly strolled into the park's camping area in the middle of the day, creating a general panic from the campers that resembled a five-alarm fire drill at an elementary school. Santa Rosa's jaguars, having enjoyed almost 20 years of continued protection, have lost some of their long-time acquired fear of people and have been sighted along beaches and rivers where they feed on turtles and other small animals. In the forests that cover the volcanoes, jaguars are more secretive and nocturnal, although recently there had been several recorded attacks on horses that were kept at the biological station.

"What do we do now?" Javier asked, his voice quiet but full of consternation. The men's spirits grew cold from dread and the chill of the falling rain. As long as the jaguar stayed on the trail it would be impossible to go through, and the horses were not about to move an inch forward. As if reading their thoughts, the jaguar stood up and, with a fluid and soundless move, disappeared into the thick vegetation by the side of the trail. There was neither the sound of branches breaking nor of leaves being crushed. As far as they knew, the jaguar could be crouching by the trail, waiting for either of them to approach. If this was the same jaguar that was killing the station's horses, it might sense a familiar smell that it associated with food.

The men turned off their flashlights. The surrounding darkness was made even darker by their blindness following the intense light. They could hear the sounds of their own hearts pumping wildly in their chests. Could the jaguar hear them, too?

The horses began to walk cautiously, their noses close to the ground. The men turned their lights back on and scanned the trail. At the place where the jaguar had entered the forest, there were tracks larger than the closed fist of a man reflected in the lights. They could be seen along the trail, a witness to the jaguar's fondness for using the open paths made by human and beast. The horses picked up the pace without any prodding from the riders. Of the jaguar, only the indelible image remained—an image that for weeks and months to come fueled stories of the men's close encounter with the most formidable predator that roams the forests of Central America.   C. DE LA R.

TAXONOMY AND RELATIVES

One of the first written references to the American jaguar comes from Amerigo Vespucci in 1500, who mentions "panthers" as one of the animals present in Venezuela (Hoogesteijn and Mondolfi, 1992). The name jaguar comes from the Tupiguaraní language (a widespread language in the Amazon and other parts of South America), which translated means "wild beast that dominates its prey in one jump." Yaguareté, another common indigenous name still in use by the Guaraní Indians of Paraguay, means "body like a dog." The species was formally described by Linnaeus in 1758, who used the common name "onza" as part of the scientific name (*Panthera onca*). Its closest relatives in Central America are the puma (*Puma concolor*), the ocelot (*Leopardus pardalis*), the margay (*Leopardus wiedii*), the tiger cat (*Leopardus tigrinus*), and the jaguarundi (*Herpailurus yaguarondi*). Its closest taxonomic relatives are the African lion (*Panthera leo*) and the Indian tiger (*Panthera tigris*). The jaguar is the third largest cat species in the world. To date, up to eight subspecies have been recognized. Recent taxonomic revisions have split the genus *Felis* into four genera, *Panthera*, *Leopardus*, *Felis*, and *Herpailurus.*

COMMON NAMES

Jaguar, tigre, tigre real, yaguar (Spanish); zac-bolay (Mayan); onça negra, yaguara pichuna (Brazil); yagua-hu, tigre negro (black jaguar), American tiger; onza (Brazil, Venezuela); yaguareté (Argentina, Paraguay).

DESCRIPTION

There is an interesting theory that explains the massive size of the jaguar.

Compared to tigers and lions, the jaguar is very similarly equipped in terms of weapons (teeth and claws) as well as raw power (strength). In continents such as Africa where there are many herding species of large prey such as antelopes, zebras, and buffaloes (common prey of lions), it is easy to explain the need to develop massive musculature and formidable weapons for overpowering them. In Central and South America, however, there are few large animals that might require such strength (tapirs and, perhaps, deer). Most of the present-day natural prey of the jaguar consists of much smaller animals such as peccaries, brocket deer, capybaras (in South America only), armadillos, agoutis, and other even smaller game, few of which travel in herds. According to the theory, when jaguars, pumas, and their extinct relative the saber-toothed cat arrived from North America during the glaciation periods, they encountered a fauna quite different from the one we have today. Gomphotheres, giant sloths, giant armadillos, mastodons, and even a species of rhinoceros populated the forests and savannas of Central America. These animals became extinct relatively recently (according to one theory, in part due to overhunting by early humans).

It is in recent times that other large prey, suitable for the jaguar's strong weaponry, arrived in the region: horses and cattle introduced by the Spaniards during the conquest of the Americas. Interestingly, jaguars are unique among the big cats in that they are the only ones that regularly kill their prey by piercing their skulls, while other species tend to prefer suffocation or strangulation methods.

Jaguars resemble the African leopards in build and coloration, although they are more robust, the head and front paws being larger and the tail shorter. In relation to its body size, it is the strongest of all cats and is able to overpower and move prey heavier and larger than itself. We observed the remains of an adult horse in northern Costa Rica that was killed by a jaguar at night in an open pasture and dragged uphill, through a barbed-wire fence, and into the forest about 100 yards. Leopards are reported to perform similar feats of strength, carrying heavy prey high into trees in order to eat undisturbed.

The coat of a jaguar is marked with black rosettes over an orange-yellow or tan background. Some jaguars have smaller spots not in the form of rosettes, and there is also a melanistic (black) version of the coat. The black jaguars (incorrectly called "black panthers") can appear in the same litter as spotted ones. However, a close look at their coats, particularly under an oblique light, reveals that the spots are still there, although hidden or masked by the dark background.

Adult jaguars can measure between 1.10 and 1.80 m from the head to the

Jaguars have the most powerful jaws in the Order Carnivora.

base of the tail, which itself can measure between 440 and 560 cm. The longest jaguar on record measured 2.7 m (including the tail). Height at the shoulder has been measured between 68 and 75 cm. Jaguars can weigh up to 158 kg, with males weighing more than females. Central American jaguars tend to be smaller and lighter than their South American counterparts, there being considerable variation in the size and weight of jaguars from Central and South America.

Jaguars have large, strong canines and massive head musculature, which makes their faces appear very round. Their eyes shine a bright greenish-yellow under a light, and their ears are small and rounded.

DENTAL FORMULA

I3/3, C1/1, P3/2, M1/1, for a total of 30 teeth.

HABITAT AND DISTRIBUTION

Jaguars inhabit a wide range of habitats, from rain forests to wet grasslands,

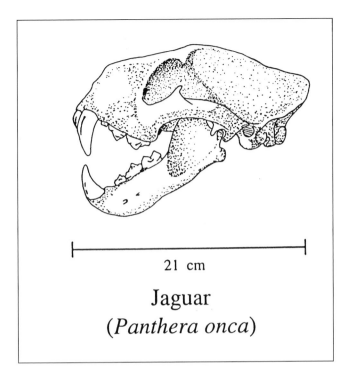

Jaguar
(*Panthera onca*)

21 cm

dry scrub lands, and even beaches. They are normally associated with bodies of water, such as rivers, streams, and lakes. Their large size requires abundant prey and large, relatively undisturbed territories in order to maintain viable populations. While jaguars will use the same habitats as pumas, pumas are usually displaced by jaguars when they occur in the same general area. They have been recorded from sea level to up to 3,800 meters in elevation, although they are usually found at less than 1,200 meters. Their range in Central America has been substantially reduced, with less than 30% of the original range still inhabited. They have become extirpated in the southwestern United States (although there has been at least one recent sighting in Arizona) and from Uruguay, so that now they are found from Mexico to Argentina.

BEHAVIOR

Jaguars are very adaptable and exhibit diurnal and nocturnal habits throughout their range. They are solitary creatures that get together only during mating season. They keep territories which they patrol and mark with urine.

Jaguars are often found resting on thick branches, especially near rivers.

They like to walk on man-made trails and are curious by nature, especially where they have not been hunted for a long time. As mentioned above, one female jaguar and her two cubs strolled into the Santa Rosa National Park camping area in the middle of the day, scattering a group of Boy Scouts and other visitors who took refuge in the park's administration building. Other jaguars have been seen walking along the beach at the same park during the early evening.

Jaguars are reported to like to rest on logs that overhang rivers, especially during the early morning hours. Karl Weidmann, a German naturalist, photographer, and filmmaker, reported (and recorded on film and in pictures) a close encounter with such a jaguar in Venezuela. It is documented in his excellent book *Fauna de Venezuela* (Weidmann, 1987). Normally shy due to overhunting, they are known to attack cattle and other livestock when desperate, usually in areas where their natural habitat has been reduced. In southern Nicaragua, for example, the combination of rapid colonization by farmers and excessive hunting of the jaguar's prey species (deer, tapirs, peccaries, agoutis, and others) has placed the remaining jaguars in a very precarious position. Seeking food, jaguars wander near settlements or farms, where they are quickly hunted down and killed by people using dogs and semi-automatic weapons.

Jaguars can roar, producing deep hoarse grunts that carry for hundreds of meters. Native jaguar hunters often imitate the call of the jaguar using a gourd or small drum over which a taut piece of rawhide has been fastened. A hole in the center, through which a string of leather or other material is passed and knotted, produces an uncannily similar series of grunts and calls which often elicit the curiosity of nearby animals. Alan Rabinowitz describes one of these callers and its use in his book *Jaguar* (Rabinowitz, 1986).

Jaguars are territorial, with the territories of males and females overlap-

3. *Historical (light) and present (dark) jaguar distribution.*

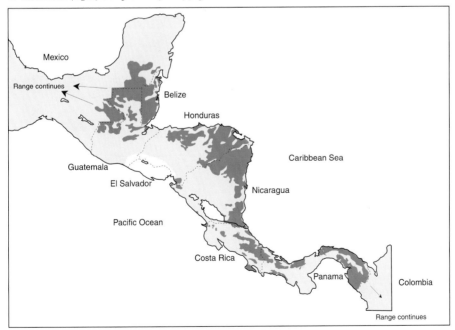

ping. A few studies have shown individual territories to be large, sometimes up to 25 square kilometers, with male territories about twice as large as those of females. It is not difficult to imagine, then, that the combination of large territorial needs and the continuing shrinkage of the jaguar's natural habitats place them in a no-win situation.

Jaguars are considered opportunistic carnivores, eating literally whatever is most abundant and easiest to catch. Besides cattle and horses, which are recent additions to the jaguar's diet, they normally feed on tapirs (*Tapirus* spp.), deer (both white-tailed and brocket deer), agoutis (*Dasyprocta punctata*), peccaries (*Tayassu tajacu*), arboreal mammals, bats, birds, fish, turtles, armadillos, anteaters, sloths, iguanas, coatis, snakes, caimans, and even fresh-water dolphins.

REPRODUCTION

Jaguars are reported to breed year-round. During mating, they copulate frequently, as much as 100 times per day, although these copulations are very short (around nine seconds each). The offspring (one or two cubs, rarely

*Young male
jaguar feeding.*

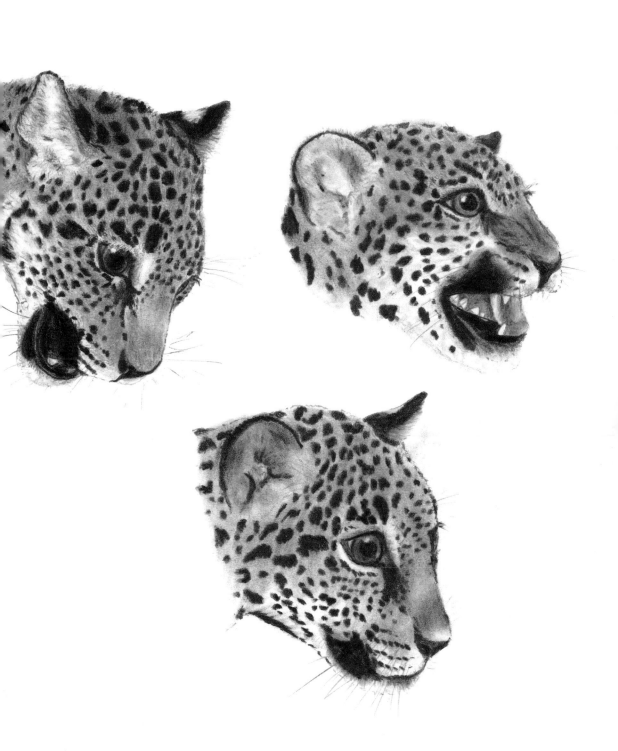

*Three facial
expressions in
a jaguar cub.*

three or even four) remain with the females until they are between 18 months and two years of age. They mature at about three years of age. Gestation lasts between 90 and 111 days, and the cubs weigh between 700 and 900 grams at birth. Cubs open their eyes after 13 days and keep the characteristic juvenile blue color of the irises almost until maturity. They den in caves, under fallen trees, in thickets, at riverbanks, under large rocks, or in other sheltered spaces. Adult females normally breed every two years.

Jaguars can live up to 11 years in nature, producing anywhere between four and eight cubs during their life span. This low rate of reproduction adds another element of risk to populations of jaguars in Central America. In captivity, jaguars have been known to live up to 23 years.

CONSERVATION STATUS

Central American jaguars have several threats, and their situation is grim in most of the region, except, perhaps, in Belize. Besides the drastic reduction of their natural range, their large territorial needs, the diminishing numbers of natural prey species, and the continuing pressure of the skin and trophy market make their plight in the region extremely serious. Habitat destruction due to the advance of agricultural frontiers is reported as the main cause of the decline of jaguar (and other feline) populations. The agricultural development carries with it other threats, such as overhunting of prey species, as well as increased hunting pressure on the jaguars themselves for their skins or because of the damage they cause to livestock. Attacks on humans are extremely rare throughout their range and clearly these attacks should not be a justification for eliminating them from a given area. Most documented attacks are from threatened, wounded, or old individual jaguars, particularly those who have lost teeth or the ability to overpower larger and faster prey.

Another serious threat to Central American jaguars is often called "the genetic factor." It has been calculated that to maintain a genetically healthy population of any animal species, a minimum number of 500 individuals should be present in a given area (Caughley and Gunn, 1996; Soulé, 1987). Given the territorial requirements and the other characteristics of jaguars, it is very difficult for them to maintain such numbers. The fragmentation of natural habitats in Central America precludes the maintenance of viable populations of jaguars in the region. Sadly, it is our opinion that free-living jaguars are doomed to disappear from most of Central America in the next 50 years or less.

Jaguars are listed under CITES Appendix I and as endangered in all of the countries in Central America except Belize. (See "The Future of Central American Carnivores" for an explanation of CITES.)

PUMA

(Puma concolor)

Adult female puma behind a tree.

Sunsets are spectacular in the dry season in Santa Rosa National Park, in northwest Costa Rica. The dry old and abandoned pastures covered with jaragua grass become deep orange as the sun approaches the horizon. This grass was introduced from Africa to Costa Rica and other Central American countries in the 1950s because of its rapid growth and its ability to produce green growth after fire during the driest months of the six-month dry season. Later, it became the bane of conservationists trying to restore the tropical dry forest that once covered this part of Costa Rica. Fires do not occur naturally in these areas of Central America, and while a useful tool for cattle ranchers, the wide expanses of grass have meant an immense challenge to those concerned with the regrowth of nonfire-adapted natural vegetation in newly protected lands. It is in this mixed habitat of gallery forest along the dry creek beds and wide expanses of jaragua grass that the puma makes its home.

I was leading a three-car expedition through the nether parts of the recently acquired expansion to the Santa Rosa Park, the Guanacaste National Park Project. A group of scientists from the Academy of Natural Sciences of Philadelphia, several prominent supporters of conservation projects from Pennsylvania, and two *National Geographic* photographers spent a week trekking by car, on foot, and by horseback through the new park lands. We were discussing plans for the development of a biological field station that would serve as the seed for a new research effort in aquatic ecology to be led by Academy scientists and local researchers. Hot, tired, and eager to arrive at Santa Rosa for a wrap-up, we turned onto the 12-kilometer macadam road to the park's main center.

I was driving the lead car on the darkening road, approaching some remnant patches of forest. I had just turned on the headlights when a large, tawny-colored animal jumped about 6 meters in front of the car from the tall grasses. Surprised, I took my foot off the accelerator and slowed down, thinking that a deer, common in the park, had been blinded by the headlights and was trying to cross the road ahead of us. But the characteristic white flash of the white-tailed deer was not there. Instead, a long, flowing tail and a very undeerlike lope replaced the original impression with a surprising one. All six passengers of the car leaned forward as the words "a puma!" were whispered in excitement.

The puma followed the road for about 50 meters, clearly visible in the bright headlights, and gave us a chance to admire its graceful run, the flow of its tail, and its muscles tensing and releasing under its short fur. It was a large male puma, with a wide, loose band of skin along its underbelly. At the next turn of the road, the puma silently leaped over a wall of grass and disappeared in the darkness.   C. DE LA R.

Aggressive expressions in an adult male puma.

TAXONOMY AND RELATIVES

Pumas are one of the six felids found in Central America. Linnaeus described the species as *Felis concolor* in 1771. Since then, it has been moved back and forth between the genera *Puma* and *Felis*. The latest literature places it into its own genus, *Puma* (Wozencraft, 1995). However, as taxonomy reflects new knowledge that is gathered on these and other species, the scientific names may suffer more changes in the future. There is one recognized subspecies in the southeastern United States (particularly in Florida). *Puma concolor cougar*, a slightly smaller subspecies, is endangered throughout its range, in spite of enormous efforts to rescue it from almost sure extinction in the wild. So far some 29 subspecies have been reported, among them *Puma concolor costaricensis*, found from Panama to Nicaragua, and *Puma concolor mayensis*, found from Mexico to Honduras.

COMMON NAMES

Puma, cougar, mountain lion, catamount, panther, painter (derived from panther) (English); léon, léon colorado, léon de montaña, león Americano (Spanish); cab-cah (Mayan); mitzli (Aztec); leopardo (Mexico); léon sabanero (Colombia); onça vermelha (Brazil); mischipichin (Ojibwa). The scientific name *concolor* means "one color" and refers to the uniformly colored fur of this animal.

DESCRIPTION

Pumas are smaller than jaguars but larger than any other cat species in Central America. Adult females have been measured between 1.5 and 2.3 m, while males can reach 2.7 m in length (not counting the tail, which can be 60 to 70 cm long). They weigh anywhere between 60 and 100 kg. Their color is generally a cinnamon or rufous brown with white or light underparts. In temperate regions, some populations tend to have grayish coloration. Young ones are spotted at birth but lose their spots at six to 12 months of age.

These cats appear longer than other cats, due to elongated necks and slim bodies. Their hind legs are longer than their front legs, which is a probable adaptation for jumping. Their heads are relatively small and their faces short, with short, rounded ears.

There is substantial variation in the pelage and coloration of pumas throughout their range, although the Central American populations tend to be rather uniform, with short, bristly fur. Melanistic pumas have only been reported from South and Central America.

Pumas have been placed in their own genus because, even though they are big cats, they also share some important characteristics with small cats. For example, pumas can purr, while jaguars and other members of the genus *Panthera* cannot. They can also "scream," or produce very high-pitched sounds, which larger cats can't. Pumas squat while they feed, while big cats tend to lie down and use their front paws to manipulate the food.

DENTAL FORMULA

I3/3, C1/1, P3/2, M1/1, for a total of 30 teeth.

HABITAT AND DISTRIBUTION

Pumas live in lowland rain forests, dry forests, and even paramos, at elevations anywhere from sea level to 5,000 meters in elevation, but are also found in coniferous forests and swamplands. They are the feline species that occupies the largest range of habitats in the Americas. The original distribution of the puma ranged from Canada to Argentina, making them the most widely distributed of the cat family in the Americas. However, North American pumas have all but disappeared in the eastern portions of the continent due to their displacement caused by intense human colonization. A subspecies known as the Florida panther or Eastern cougar, *Felis concolor cougar*, survives in Florida and in a few other locations. Presently, it is more common in the western United States. In Central America, pumas occupy just about every life zone, from deforested and grass-covered lowlands, to grassland and thick rain forest habitats up to elevations of over 3,000 meters.

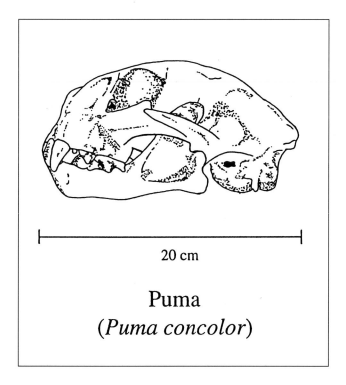

20 cm

Puma
(*Puma concolor*)

Puma resting on a tree.

BEHAVIOR

Pumas are very efficient hunters. They can outrun a deer for short distances, but prefer stalking and pouncing on their intended prey. They can leap 6 to 10 meters in a pounce. Their hunting and killing techniques for large prey are similar to those of other cats: grab shoulders and neck with the front paws, dig in the hind claws on the sides, and bite and crush the bones on the back of the neck. Usually, they drag the carcass to a sheltered spot and gorge, eating the internal organs first (liver, heart, and lungs, entering through the stomach). Then they cover the uneaten parts with litter. They return to their cache for several days until finished. Pumas feed on white-tailed and brocket deer (*Odocoileus virginianus* and *Mazama americana*, respectively), porcu-

Female puma carrying a cub.

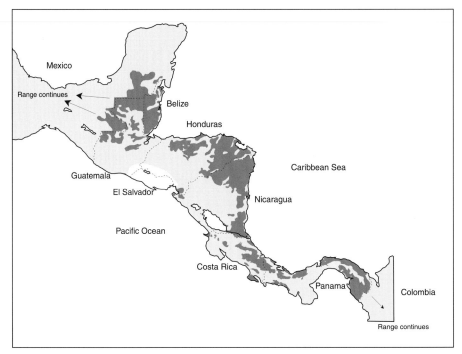

4. *Historical (light) and present (dark) puma distribution.*

pines, raccoons, mice, livestock, coyotes, agoutis, armadillos, and tamanduas (a Central American species of anteater). They also eat grass and a few insects.

They mark their territories with mounds of forest litter which they soak regularly with urine or feces. Males also make scratches or scrapes along paths and under trees or ledges. Their scat is copious, usually formed of irregular tubes or pellets within which one can find hair and crushed bones. As in other species of cats (including our domesticated friends), they tend to cover their scat, at least partially, with litter.

Pumas tend to avoid places where jaguars live, although they share many similar habitats and prey. Their wider range of habitats allows them to replace jaguars as the top predator in many places.

REPRODUCTION

Pumas produce usually one litter every two years, having anywhere between one and rarely up to six cubs. Usual litter sizes are two or three kittens. They breed year-round, with a gestation period of about 93 days (perhaps shorter in the tropics). The young stay with the mother for about two years. Dens are relatively simple places with little cover, usually found under rock outcrops, in niches, or under fallen trees. Females usually have their first litter at about three years of age.

CONSERVATION STATUS

Pumas are listed under CITES Appendix I in the United States and as endangered throughout most of their range. They are hunted as a game animal in some western states where their populations are not threatened. Most of the knowledge we presently have about the species comes from studies done in temperate regions, but there is relatively little known about the habits and general ecology of the species in the tropics. The Florida panther is seriously threatened, and much effort has been made to save the wild population, even to the point of introducing "fresh genetic stock" from Texas and Arizona. Loss of habitat and overhunting threaten the species throughout Central America.

Pumas rarely attack people, although they are known to attack cattle and other domestic animals with some regularity, which makes them targets for extirpation by ranchers and farmers. Recently, in the United States there have been several confirmed human deaths caused by puma attacks.

OCELOT
(Leopardus pardalis)

Three little boys were standing outside the gate shouting for Elías, the station's main cat caretaker, to come out. Elías was out cleaning the cages and feeding the cats, so I went to find out what all the excitement was about. I was working as a volunteer at the newly established National Center for Feline Rescue, PROFELIS, at a station that took care of the many small wild cats that were turned in to Costa Rica's Wildlife Service. The station was created to support endangered feline research as well as to provide a holding facility for confiscated animals. We hoped some could be eventually released back into the wild. During the first year of operation, the station was home to a full house of nearly 40 ocelots, margays, and jaguarundis.

It took me a while to understand in all the commotion what had happened. Apparently the kids had been working in the fields with their father when their dog had found an ocelot and chased it up a tree. The kids were very excited and wanted us to "catch their ocelot and put it in a cage." I explained to the boys that we didn't catch wild animals and that "their" ocelot belonged to the wild. Still, a wild ocelot sighting was an interesting event. Elías, who just had returned and was helping me interpret the rapid-fire Spanish of the boys, went along to check if the ocelot had been hurt by the dog.

After twenty minutes of walking through pastures and tangled shrubs, we met the father of the boys, who was standing under a tree close to a small lake near the village. He had a tiny dog with him that obviously could not have done any harm to the ocelot. We looked up and found a frightened female ocelot staring down at us. She was a beautiful dark-orange color. We enjoyed watching her, while giving the kids and their father little tidbits of information about these animals and their importance in the balance of nature. After a while, we all left so she could calm down and leave.   c. c. n.

Ocelots are large and powerful cats which are seldom encountered in the wild. My first close encounter with an ocelot was at PROFELIS with a female that had been raised in captivity and was now a fully grown adult. She was the star of the station. Having been raised by humans, Taffa was very tame and playful, seeking, and even needing, the company of people. Owning ocelots—or any other endangered species—is illegal in Costa Rica, so she had been confiscated by officers of the Wildlife Service and delivered to the station a few months back. She enjoyed a very large cage near the main house, and her habits were mostly diurnal. She spent a lot of time playing with special "toys" brought to her daily by the caretakers of the station. These toys consisted of banana-plant leaves, which Taffa energetically shredded to pieces every day, a coconut hung on a sturdy manila rope, and thick branches, which she climbed and from which she "stalked" visitors to her tiny realm.

Upon entering the cage, Taffa quickly accepted me as a new playmate, climbed onto my lap, and curled herself around my arm, biting at my exposed skin. She was surprisingly heavy. Her incredibly soft fur confirmed the main reason why these cats have been hunted to near extinction throughout most of their range. Her enormous paws seemed too large for her slim body. They were evidence of the Spanish name commonly given to this species, "Manigordo," or "fat hands." While Taffa joyously gnawed my arm, I inspected the large paws with half-inch–long retractable claws, which she sharpened on the branches scattered through her cage. Her sandpaper tongue could easily strip the hair from my arms. Covered in saliva and rather battered by the exercise, I exited the cage, having gained a healthy respect for this amazing hunter of tropical and subtropical America.

*Adult ocelot playing
on a branch.*

On a recent trip to Nicaragua, I was amazed to find in one of shops at the International Airport a leather purse adorned with a wide band of ocelot skin. I asked the shop's attendant who would buy these purses, telling her that most countries would not allow the entrance of these items, and that they would be immediately confiscated. She smiled and said that American and European tourists were very fond of these gifts, and that she recommended that they bury the items deep in their luggage to avoid detection by customs officials. I also found ocelot and margay skins—and even a whole mounted ocelot—in the famous Artisan's Market in Masaya, southwest of the capital city of Managua. Although endangered and protected throughout the region, including Nicaragua, lax controls still allow an active commerce with these animals.   C. DE LA R.

TAXONOMY AND RELATIVES

The ocelot, *Leopardus pardalis*, was formally described by Linnaeus in 1758 but with a different genus name (*Felis pardalis*). It is closely related to the margay (*L. wiedii*) and the tiger cat (*L. tigrinus*) and is the largest of the three. It is one of the four species of spotted cats of Central America. This species— as well as its closest relatives—has been moved back and forth among various genera, particularly the genus *Felis*, but also the genera *Margay* (by Gray in 1867), *Oncilla* (by Allen in 1919), *Oncoides* (by Severtzov in 1858) and *Pardalis* (again by Gray in 1867). At the species level there are many synonyms as well. So far 11 subspecies have been described.

Portrait of a female ocelot. Face patterns in all spotted cats are unique.

Adult male ocelot growling.
Compare facial markings
with previous figure.

Fossil ocelots have been found in Florida and in Central and South America, particularly those who lived at the end of the Pleistocene (Werdelin, 1985).

COMMON NAMES

Ocelot; ocelote, ozelot (German); manigordo (Costa Rica, Nicaragua, Panama, Venezuela); tigrillo, gato tigre (Panama); tigre chico (Panama); cunaguaro (Venezuela); xacxícin (Mexico, of Mayan origin); maracaya (Colombia). The name "tigrillo," which means "little tiger" in Spanish, is erroneously applied to this and other species, including newborn and juvenile jaguars. The true "tigrillo" is the tiger cat (*Leopardus tigrinus*).

DESCRIPTION

The ocelot is the second largest spotted cat in Central America. With a head-body length (without tail) of approximately 70 to 100 cm, it is considerably smaller than the jaguar. In contrast to the jaguar, which has a very muscular and heavy body, the ocelot is leaner and much lighter, allowing a more arboreal mode of living. Females weigh between 8 and 9 kg, while males weigh up to 12 or occasionally even 15 kg. Ocelots don't have regular round spots. Instead, on the neck and body they possess a pattern of elongated black rosettes or stripes over a background that can vary between yellow, tan, or sometimes nearly white, particularly around the belly and the inside of the legs. Black individuals can sometimes be seen, though they are rare. As in the other spotted cats, their faces show a pattern of spots and stripes that is very distinct, and individuals can easily be recognized. As the Spanish name (manigordo) suggests, their feet are big in proportion to their bodies, and the fore paws are broader than the hind paws.

Another interesting characteristic is that the fur around the neck area slants forward and presents black lines. Their eyes shine a very bright light yellow. Ocelots present a convex muzzle when viewed on profile.

DENTAL FORMULA
I3/3, C1/1, P3/2, M1/1, for a total of 30 teeth.

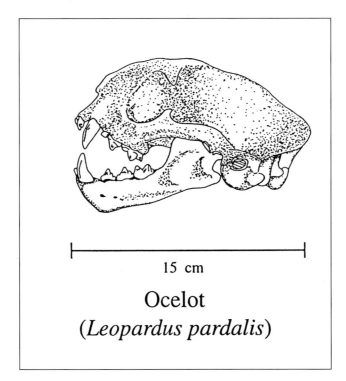

15 cm

Ocelot
(*Leopardus pardalis*)

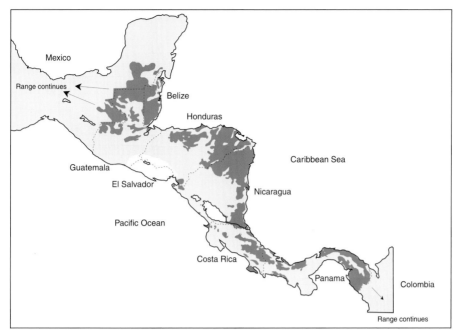

5. *Historical (light) and present (dark) ocelot distribution.*

HABITAT AND DISTRIBUTION

Ocelots inhabit a wide variety of habitats, including primary and secondary rain forests and dry forests, as well as gallery forests (along streams and rivers), usually at elevations of 1,200 meters and below, although one source reports them at elevations up to 3,800 meters (Gomes de Oliveira, 1994). Basically, any dense-cover habitat seems to be suitable to ocelots, and their presence in a given place seems to be dependent on both adequate cover and prey density. They are present in North, Central, and South America, from south Texas to northern Argentina. Very few studies have been carried out on their territorial requirements. Estimates for males' ranges are from 3.5 to 17.7 square kilometers, and for females', between 1.1 and 14.6 square kilometers; the territories of the male generally overlap the territories of several females.

BEHAVIOR

Ocelots are mostly nocturnal and crepuscular, but they are occasionally seen in the daytime. They normally move and hunt alone. Their presence in a given area is indicated by their tracks and by the latrines where they defecate on a regular basis. They feed on rodents, birds, lizards, snakes, and even amphibians and fish. In reality, anything small that moves captures their interest. Although they normally hunt on the ground, they also hunt in trees, as they are good climbers and often rest or sleep on branches. It has been reported that ocelots eat their prey starting with the head if the prey is small and with the belly if it is large. Actually, ocelots vary in their feeding habits; while some individuals may feed this way, others manipulate their prey differently. Some skin, pluck, or dehair the animal before eating it, while others will eat the hair and feathers. Ocelots normally stay near their kills until the prey is fully eaten, covering the leftovers with forest litter and returning to them until they are gone. These leftovers normally consist of skins, large bones, feathers, and entrails. They are fond of man-made trails, which are good places to look for their tracks.

Ocelots do not roar but are very vocal. They emit various meows and screams, especially during mating season. Females in heat can be very loud.

REPRODUCTION

Female ocelots begin to breed at the age of 18 to 22 months and can breed until 13 years of age. Males mature sexually at about 15 months. Estrous occurs every four to six months and lasts between five and seven days. They breed year-round, copulating five to ten times per day. If conception occurs, the gestation period lasts between 70 and 80 days. They have one to two young about every two years and the female takes care of the young which stay with her for up to a year. During lactation and caring of the young, the

Male ocelot resting.

Claudia Hocke '95

*Face of young
male ocelot.*

activity of females increases dramatically due to the increased need to obtain food for the young. Young ones reach adult size at about eight to 10 months of age, and sexual maturity at about 18 to 22 months.

CONSERVATION STATUS

At one time, ocelots were one of the main spotted cat skin imports into the United States, numbers sometimes reaching over 140,000 ocelot skins per year. It took 13 or 14 ocelot skins to make one fur coat, and two or three to make a handbag. Even though they are fully protected today in most countries, one can still buy a purse with ocelot skin decorations in the Managua International Airport and in local artisan markets.

Like other Central American cats, ocelots are endangered throughout their range and are listed under CITES Appendix I. Many countries totally prohibit their hunting. However, actual protection is lax in many countries, and there is an active black market for ocelot and other spotted cat skins in the region. Although many protected areas might hold viable populations of ocelots, their dwindling numbers and isolation work against them. In areas where encroachment and habitat destruction impinge on their range, they begin to kill and eat poultry, further aggravating their status.

MARGAY

(Leopardus wiedii)

Adult female margay sitting on a tree branch.

Early mornings on the side of an extinct volcano in Costa Rica can be very wet indeed. Water dripped from every available leaf in fat, heavy drops that made a soft splashing sound when they hit the waterlogged forest floor. The narrow muddy trail crossed the little stream I was studying, and I turned left at the crossing, beginning the dangerous climb along its shore. Stepping carefully from rock to slippery rock, I sought the support of the overhanging branches and small trees, always wary of the nearly perfect camouflage of the eyelash vipers (*Bothriechis schlegelii*) that made their homes along these tropical streams.

At one turn of the stream I ran face to face with a margay busy with something on the ground. At the sight of me, the margay bolted and silently disappeared in the stream-side vegetation. I barely caught a glimpse of the creature, with its black spots on a buffy-yellow background, its size scarcely bigger than a large house cat, its enormous eyes, no doubt well-adapted for nighttime hunting, and its long flowing tail.

After my heart returned to normal speed, I looked for the object of the margay's interest, which I found at the base of a large tree. The margay had been feeding on a porcupine's carcass stripped of its quill-studded skin, which now lay crumpled about a meter away. I gingerly picked up the skin and examined it. The work appeared almost surgical. After killing the porcupine (or perhaps finding it dead already), the margay had made a long incision along its belly, the least spiny region of its body, and had peeled away the skin toward the back and the head. Then it had severed the head and each of the paws and had lifted the skinless and quill-free body to eat at ease.

I had read a report of a semitame margay who had had the worse part of an encounter with a porcupine, taking with it a face and neck full of quills (Koford, 1983). However, in spite of their formidable defense, porcupines do have weak spots and can fall prey to an experienced and careful predator. This seemed to have been one of those times, for the carcass was very fresh and still bloody.

I collected the skin and returned to the site about two hours later to find the porcupine body gone, only its entrails left semiburied in the wet leaves. To this day, every time I pull out the porcupine skin to show students at a talk—and invariably get pricked by one or more of the sharp quills—I still marvel at the margay's skill at killing and handling this most formidably defended inhabitant of the tropical forest.   C. DE LA R.

TAXONOMY AND RELATIVES

Margays were first described in 1821 by Schinz under the genus *Felis*. Schinz named this cat "wiedii" in honor of the Prince of Wied. Margays' closest relatives are ocelots (*L. pardalis*) and tiger cats (*L. tigrinus*). They were formerly placed in the genus *Felis*, but, as mentioned above, recent taxonomic revisions have split the genus *Felis* into the genera *Panthera, Leopardus, Felis,* and *Herpailurus.* There is also a number of subspecies in these genera, but scientists have not yet reached a full agreement on taxonomy for the Neotropical branch of this family.

COMMON NAMES

Margay, little or tree ocelot; tigrillo, gato tigre (Spanish); tigrillito (Belize); pichigüeta (Mexico); caucel (Costa Rica, Honduras); mabaracaya (Guatemala); chulul (Mayan); gato pintado, huamburushu, cunaguaro (Venezuela); Baumozelot, Langschwanzkatze (German).

DESCRIPTION

The margay is one of the four species of spotted cats found in Central America. It is perhaps the most common of them in spite of having been heavily persecuted for its soft and beautifully patterned skin. A full-grown margay

Young male margay playing with a stick.

Female margay sunning on a branch.

can weigh up to 5 kg and measure up to 79 cm from the tip of its nose to the base of its tail, a size intermediate between the ocelot (up to 1 m) and the tiger cat (up to 55 cm). Female margays tend to be smaller than males; margays, in general, are larger than house cats. In proportion to their body size, their tails are longer than those of ocelots, which is believed to aid them in their arboreal acrobatics.

Their body color ranges from tawny yellow to grayish brown (depending on where they live), with rows of black spots and blotches on the body and heavy black stripes on the neck. There is much individual variation among spotted cats, and margays are no exception. Like ocelots, their neck hair grows in reverse toward the head. As in all spotted cats, individuals can be easily distinguished by their unique facial and body color patterns. Their fur is thick and soft, another reason for its demand in the fur trade. Their very large eyes distinguish them from their closest relatives. When illuminated at night, their eyes shine very bright and yellowish. An important characteristic is their rotating ankle joint, which allows them unusual tree-climbing ability. It is interesting to note that margays, ocelots, and tiger cats have 36 chromosomes, while most of the other cats have 38.

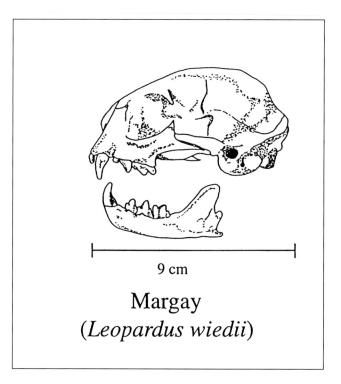

Margay
(*Leopardus wiedii*)

9 cm

DENTAL FORMULA

I3/3, C1/1, P3/2, M1/1, for a total of 30 teeth.

HABITAT AND DISTRIBUTION

Margays are usually found in dense forests from southern Texas to southern Brazil at elevations below 3,000 meters, although in Central America they rarely go above 1,200 meters. They have been reported from humid forests, rain forests, evergreen forests, swamps (such as the Brazilian pantanal), savannas, and other habitats. They are also known to use gallery forests (along streams and rivers), as well as small patches of vegetation between larger tracts of undisturbed forest. They are the most arboreal of Central American cats, foraging in the trees for rodents and birds, although they also hunt on the ground. They are considered rare throughout their range, but we believe this is because they are seldom seen due to their nocturnal habits. They seem to have adapted well to disturbed habitats, even thriving in disturbed forests near human habitation.

BEHAVIOR

Margays are superbly adapted to an arboreal life. Their long tail—longer than

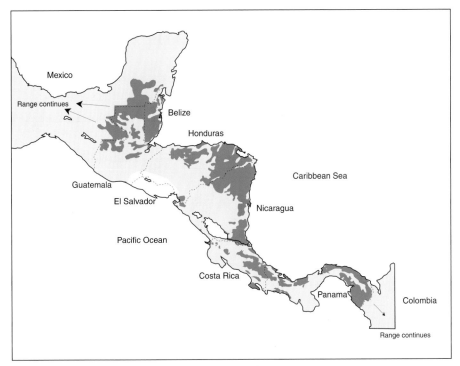

6. *Historical (light) and present (dark) margay distribution.*

any of the other species' tails in relation to their bodies—is believed to act as a counterweight while the margay moves along branches of trees. Unique to margays is the ability to rotate their feet at their ankles, which allows them to hang upside down from branches or to descend trees face down, clinging to the bark as a squirrel does. Margays rest and sleep in trees, usually seven to 10 meters above the ground. They are solitary animals, moving and hunting mostly at night. Males and females mark territories which overlap; the territory area depends on the availability of food and mating opportunities. They use urine spraying sites, facial rubbings, and scratching posts to mark the limits of these territories, and both males and females protect them against individuals of their own sex. Sightings of more than one margay together usually indicate relatedness or mating pairs. In captivity they can easily be kept in pairs. They behave very socially and will groom each other, sleep together, and play extensively.

Margays are strictly carnivorous and eat prey ranging from small mammals, birds, reptiles, amphibians, and insects, to eggs. They obtain most of their prey in trees. As with most felines and canids, they also eat grass, which helps them regurgitate excess stomach acid and hair balls.

*Female margay
climbing down
a tree.*

REPRODUCTION

Margays usually give birth to one kitten—rarely twins—a year, with a gestation period of about 75 days (although Gomes de Oliveira, 1994, reports gestation periods between 81 and 84 days). The young weigh about 450 g, four times as much as newborn domestic cats. They have uniform black spots, and, like many other cats, they have blue eyes until the age of four to six weeks. Young are reared solely by the mother; although the weaning age has not been fully determined, it is believed to be about eight months. There has been little field research done on wild margays, so we don't know many aspects of their life history. In captivity, margays reproduce well and tend to become more social and tolerant of other margays than in nature. Sexual maturity is reached at around two years of age, although they look full grown at about nine to 12 months. It is important to stress that data on reproduction, ages of sexual maturity, development, and growth are usually reported for captive individuals. There is probably a greater variation in the wild than with what we see in captive animals whose diet and habitats are clearly different.

*Young male and
female margays
playing.*

Juvenile margay sleeping.

CONSERVATION STATUS

As all other species of the family Felidae, margays are endangered through-out much of their range, and they are placed in CITES Appendix I. Besides hunting—which is outlawed in most Central American countries—habitat destruction is the biggest threat to this species. Even today they are still ille-gally hunted for their fur, and it takes about 15 dead margays to make one human fur coat. Pet trade has also played a role in diminishing margay popu-lations. It is believed that margays are easily tamed and that they make good pets. However, a full-grown margay can be very damaging to furniture and human skin alike. Besides, their mostly nocturnal habits are not easily com-patible with those of humans. Wild cats in general can seldom be fully do-mesticated and do not make good pets.

TIGER CAT

(Leopardus tigrinus or tigrina)

I have stopped at Las Pumas ranch in the Guanacaste Province, Costa Rica, at least 50 times in the last 10 years. Over the years, Lilly and Werner Hagnauer have become good friends, and I stopped in at their farm and animal rescue station to say hello and to see what new additions to the extended family they had. Huracán's cage, housing the large Brazilian jaguar, was one of my usual stops. I had taken pictures of him over the years and used them in magazine articles and in my talks. Huracán and Tiki, the younger Nicaraguan jaguar, were also film stars, having been featured in several TV shows.

Another regular stop was at Robby's cage; he was a tiger cat that I had never seen outside of his hiding place, because he liked to sleep inside a hollow log near the top of the cage, about three meters above the floor. From there he could survey the trail that wound around the miniature zoo and sleep undisturbed by people walking around. I tried many more times than I care to remember to get a good photo of Robby, but the only pictures I was able to get were of his face framed by the hollow log. Once, I got a picture of his tail; the log with a yellow-and-black tail sticking out hung near my desk for many years.

Robby, like most tiger cats, was active at night. He would leave his hideout to eat, stretch his legs, and then, at first light, climb back into the safety and darkness of his log. I often wondered if these strictly nocturnal habits lead us to believe that this species is more rare than it actually is. If you have ever seen a tiger cat in the wild, consider yourself very lucky, for this small, shy cat is extremely endangered and increasingly rare.   C. DE LA R.

TAXONOMY AND RELATIVES

The tiger cat was first described by Schreber in 1775 as a new species of the genus *Felis*. It was later placed into *Leopardus* by Allen in 1919 and, as with the other small cats, has flipped back and forth between genera (*Felis* and *Oncifelis*) since then. Its closest relatives are the ocelot (*L. pardalis*) and the margay (*L. wiedii*), both larger than the tiger cat. Emmons (1990) and Eisenberg (1989), two important references on Neotropical mammals, as well as other sources, call this species *Felis tigrina*, a probable synonym of the species name (Wozencraft, 1995; Nowell et al., 1995). Emmons (1997) corrected the name to *Leopardus tigrinus*.

COMMON NAMES

Tiger cat, oncilla, little tiger cat, little spotted cat (English); chat tigre, oncille (French); Onzille, Kleinfleckenkatze, Zwergtigerkatze (German); tigrillo, tigrica, gato tigre (Spanish); tigrillo (Costa Rica); tigrito (Venezuela); tigrillo peludo, tigre gallinero (Colombia). As it can be seen, many of the common names for this species overlap with those of margays, with which tiger cats are often confused.

DESCRIPTION

Tiger cats look very similar to small margays and the two species are very difficult to tell apart in the field. Tiger cats look very much like small house cats, weighing about 2.2 kg. Their body length ranges from 44 to 65 cm, and the tail measures from 25 to 33 cm. Their tails are proportionally shorter than their bodies (about 56% of the head and body length) when compared to the margay's, although this is hardly a useful field characteristic. Their fur is not as plush as the margay's (in some individuals it is quite rough), and the

Adult tiger cat resting on a tree.

hair on the neck does not grow forward as in ocelots and margays. Spots and rosettes are lighter and less blotchy than those of margays. Colors range from yellows and tawny browns to almost gray individuals. The small spots and rosettes are often tiny. Black individuals have been found and appear to be quite common.

Their tracks are nearly indistinguishable from those of house cats, thus making them difficult to document in areas near settlements.

DENTAL FORMULA
I3/3, C1/1, P3/2, M1/1, for a total of 30 teeth.

HABITAT AND DISTRIBUTION
Tiger cats seem to prefer higher elevations than margays, although their ranges overlap widely. They have been found in lowland forests and premontane forests, both primary and secondary. In Colombia they have been encountered at elevations up to 4,500 meters near or at the snow line (Melquist, 1984), although they probably do not venture much into those elevations. They have also been collected in cloud forests in Costa Rica (Gardner, 1971). Their present northernmost range appears to be northern Costa Rica. Their range extends into South America to northern Argentina. More field research is needed to document the range of this species.

BEHAVIOR
Very little is known about the habits and behaviors of tiger cats in the wild,

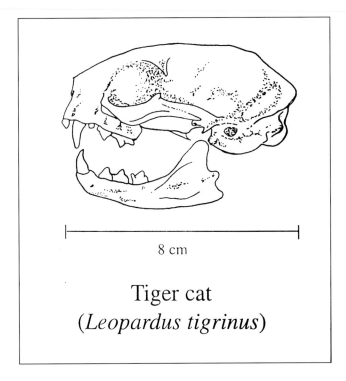

Tiger cat
(Leopardus tigrinus)

since no studies have been conducted on this species. Information from captive specimens and a few ancillary observations (Gomes de Oliveira, 1994) suggests that they have primarily nocturnal habits. They are good climbers but appear to prefer hunting on the ground. Most observations of their feeding habits come from stomach content analysis of a few captured specimens. They eat rodents and small birds, insects, lizards, bird eggs, and even small primates (in Brazil). Practically nothing is known of their home ranges or territories, use of their habitats, or habits. They are reported to adapt well to disturbed and suburban areas and even have been reported from metropolitan areas in Brazil.

REPRODUCTION

All of the information on the reproduction of tiger cats comes from observation of captive animals. Sexual maturity seems to be reached at two to two-and-a-half years of age. There have been suggestions that tiger cats mate for life and that the male participates in the care and protection of the kittens (Widholzer et al., 1981; Gomes de Oliveira, 1994). They den in hollow trees or under logs, and have been observed resting high in trees. Their gestation

*Face of a
very young
tiger cat.*

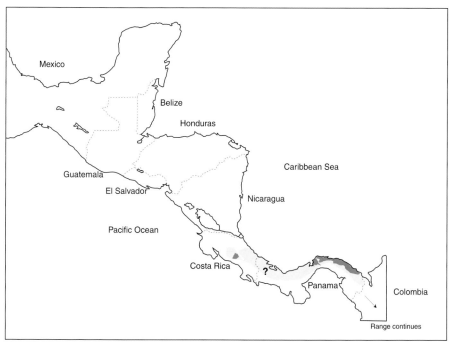

7. *Historical (light) and present (dark) tiger cat distribution.*

*Young tiger cat
on a tree fork.*

period has been reported from 55 days up to 78 days. Most of the time one kitten is born, although sometimes twins. Kittens open their eyes at one to two weeks from birth and begin taking solid food after a month to a month-and-a-half. They achieve almost full adult size at 11 months (Gomes de Oliveira, 1994).

CONSERVATION STATUS

Tiger cats are listed under CITES Appendix I. Hunting is prohibited in Costa Rica as well as in most of South America. The species is legally unprotected in Panama and Nicaragua, a status that probably will change very soon. Deforestation and habitat loss seem to be the greatest threats to tiger cats. The pelt market has been substantial in South America, but little is known about the collection and trade of tiger cat skins in Central America. It is likely that tiger cats are lumped with margays in the hunting and skin trading statistics.

JAGUARUNDI

(Herpailurus yaguarondi)

Trusting your main water supply to a four-inch pipe stuck in a river is an iffy arrangement, especially in the rainy season. The Maritza Biological Field Station, high on the slopes of Orosí volcano in northern Costa Rica, originally had this setup. Over one kilometer of PVC tubing had been laid at great expense in sweat and effort through the forest from the station's buildings to a pool on the upper reaches of the Tempisquito River. The arrangement worked fine during the dry season, for the water level was fairly constant and the water crystalline. However, when the rains began, large quantities of leaves, sticks, and sand would find their way to the inlet, plugging it. Flash floods, strong enough to move Volkswagen Beetle–sized boulders, would play havoc with our rudimentary system, requiring constant supervision and maintenance. Deep in the primary forests of the volcano, the regular maintenance trips were made less of a chore by numerous encounters with wildlife.

I tried to take my photographic equipment on these trips, as I was often rewarded by unique photo opportunities. This time, however, the continuous rain of a "temporal," a several-day stretch of foul weather, precluded these distractions, so my trip to the water intake was pure business.

*Red phase
jaguarundi
growling.*

Murphy's Law is unbending in these situations. On my way back from the backbreaking pipe repair, I stopped at the sight of three sunbitterns (*Eurypyga helias*) displaying their bright wing patterns—resembling setting suns with rainbows over them—to each other on the boulders that protruded from the stream channel. From my hiding place behind some bushes above the small canyon, I could see the sunbitterns totally engrossed with their display, necks down, wings spread, sunsets all around.

Suddenly, they all stopped and turned their attention toward a log that crossed the stream above their heads. A large jaguarundi had made a soundless approach from the opposite shore and was now perched right above the birds. The jaguarundi was no more than 10 meters from where I was hiding.

I cursed my bad luck at having a hammer, a pipe wrench, and some duct tape as my only equipment. The jaguarundi seemed to weigh his options below, while the birds were frozen in the middle of their spread-eagle displays. The swollen stream rushed noisily under the log, and the boulder tips where the birds perched appeared awfully small for an attempt at a jump. A fall into the foamy current could be dangerous, even to an agile jaguarundi. Caution seemed to be the best option, as the jaguarundi began to walk back to the other shore, its position followed as if by radar antennas by the still spread-winged birds. Once out of sight, the birds called it quits and flew upstream to safer grounds.   C. DE LA R.

There were a lot of growling noises coming out of the small wooden box that had just arrived at the station. Peeking inside, all I could see were two hissing and spitting little dark fur balls in the weak light of the approaching dusk. Working with head lamps, we prepared a small thick-wire cage near the house for our two new guests. I was quite curious about what I would see once the box was opened, but the two dark "fur balls" were very shy and kept hissing in their box, which was now sitting in one corner of the cage. It was not until the next day that I had a better look at "The Twins," as the two jaguarundi kittens were christened. It was difficult to tell them apart, and they didn't lose their shyness until they were much older.

Jaguarundis are very shy wild cats, even those that have been kept in captivity for a long time. The two new arrivals to the PROFELIS Cat Rescue Center were brought to us by a farmer who claimed to have found them "abandoned" by their mother. Most likely, the mother was off hunting for their meal, for the babies were old enough to eat solid food. These were the first jaguarundis that had arrived at the station, and having had little contact with humans (that is, they had not been tamed), they stayed fairly shy. This could be a good case for releasing them back into the wild.

About one year later the decision on what should happen to the two jaguarundis was made for us at the cat station. Hurricane Caesar hit the station at their new location in Uvita de Dominical. It struck by night and a new river started to run right through the cages. Within minutes it was growing bigger and bigger. The only thing to do to save the less tame animals was to open their cages and to release them into the wild. The twins, now grown up, stood a good chance to survive and prosper in the wild.   C. C. N.

TAXONOMY AND RELATIVES

Jaguarundis (*Herpailurus yaguarondi*) were first described by Lacépède in

1809 under the genus *Felis*. The species name is often spelled *yagouaroundi* (e.g., in Emmons, 1990; corrected in the 1997 edition), which is not an accepted name (Wozencraft, 1995), or *yaguaroundi*, which is considered a synonym (Wozencraft, 1995). The genus *Herpailurus* is considered by some sources as a subgenus of *Felis*. Their closest relatives in Central America are the small spotted cats of the genus *Leopardus* (the ocelot, the margay, and the tiger cat), although evolutionarily speaking, they are more related to Old World species. They probably invaded the Americas through the Bering land bridge together with the ancestors of the puma (Werdelin, 1985). The species is only known from a recent fossil record dating from near the end of the Pleistocene.

COMMON NAMES

Jaguarundi, yaguarundi, otter cat (English); jaguarundi (French); Jaguarundi, Wieselkatze, Eyra (German); onza, gato moro, gato eyra (Spanish); halari (Belize); gato pardo, gato servante, ulama (Colombia); león breñero (Costa Rica); tejón, mabaracaya-eira (Guatemala); gato cerbán (Honduras); ekmuch (Mayan); tigrillo congo, tigrillo negro (Panama); gato cervantes (Venezuela).

DESCRIPTION

Jaguarundis look the least like cats of all the felines, and they are often confused with tayras (*Eira barbara*), weasels (although weasels in Central America are much smaller), and even otters (which are much larger than jaguarundis). They possess an elongated body and face, and a very long tail. Their walk is fast and weasel-like, hence the confusion. They also come in two color phases, once believed to be two different species until captive breeding showed both phases in the same litters (Kitchener, 1991). There is considerable variation in both color phases. One is generally uniformly dark gray or grizzled gray; the other is usually reddish or cinnamon, with variation toward yellower, paler colors or brown; and both phases are lighter on the underbellies, often showing some spotting (but no stripes or rosettes as in its spotted relatives). Emmons (1997) reports that rain forest animals tend to be dark brown or black, while individuals from dryer areas tend to be yellowish-brown or red. Both colors appear in the same population.

Their bodies are long and slender, larger and longer than those of house cats, and they weigh around 6 kg. Their bodies measure between 60 and 75 cm, with tails between 30 and 46 cm long. They have long necks, thin faces,

small heads, shortish legs, and very long tails. The pupils are round like those of the genus *Panthera*.

DENTAL FORMULA

I3/3, C1/1, P3/2, M1/1, for a total of 28 to 30 teeth (the first pair of premolars may be very reduced or absent).

HABITAT AND DISTRIBUTION

Jaguarundis are found from the southern United States (particularly in Texas) to northern Argentina, usually at elevations below 2,200 meters. They inhabit gallery forests, evergreen and dry deciduous forests, rain forests, scrub, and secondary vegetation. They can adapt to disturbed areas and prey on poultry and other small farm animals. They appear to be less common in rain forest habitats. Dense gallery forests and edge habitats seem to be good places for jaguarundis. Their mostly daytime habits make them more visible to humans than the other species of cats.

Black phase jaguarundi. Notice the long tail.

BEHAVIOR

These animals are diurnal and crepuscular, although they are also active at night. While their tendency is to hunt on the ground, they can climb trees and move easily among branches in search of prey or resting areas. They are very agile and fast, and can perform some near-incredible acrobatics to reach prey. The pair of twin jaguarundis that arrived at the PROFELIS station performed spectacular somersaults and jumps at feeding time. The caretakers would throw chicken wings onto the roof of the cage, and the jaguarundis would run up a branch, jump high into the air, and hold on with one paw to the wire mesh while scooping down the food morsel. Then they would drop to the ground, very catlike, onto their feet, scampering to a hidden spot to eat it.

In the wild, jaguarundis appear to prefer ground-dwelling birds to small mammals, although they will eat whatever is available, including rodents, reptiles, birds, insects, arthropods, and fish stranded in mud puddles. They are frequently observed traveling in pairs (Nowell et al., 1995).

They appear to be aggressive but shy. Approaching the cage of captive jaguarundis always elicits the same response from them: hissing and teeth-

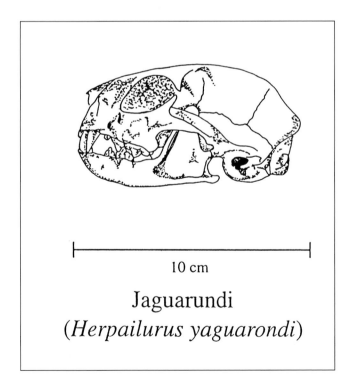

10 cm

Jaguarundi
(*Herpailurus yaguarondi*)

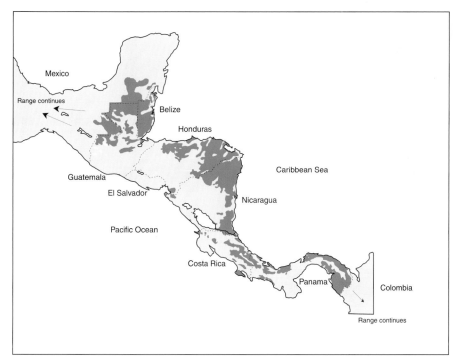

8. *Historical (light) and present (dark) jaguarundi distribution.*

baring from a crouched position, no matter how habituated to people they seem to be. They also seem very energetic and mobile. Their home range has been calculated around 100 square kilometers, almost twice as large as that of a jaguar! They also feed copiously, up to 0.6 kg a day. In human terms, this is equivalent to a normal adult eating about 6 kg of food every day.

Jaguarundis seem to be among the most vocal of all cat species. Some 13 different vocalizations have been recorded, among which the most impressive is a birdlike whistle and chirping noise, which is very hard to recognize as a cat call. Very little research has been carried out on this species, either in the field or in captivity, so it is the least-known of all Central American felids.

REPRODUCTION

Observations of captive individuals have shown that females roll on their backs and deposit small amounts of urine in various places while softly calling and making various vocalizations. During mating, the male mounts the female from behind, biting her neck while copulating, which is a typical cat behavior. Mating is often accompanied by loud screaming by the female toward the end of the copula.

Jaguarundis are late bloomers, achieving sexual maturity after one-and-a-

Red male jaguarundi playing.

Profile of a young jaguarundi.

half to three years of age (in captive animals), with the females maturing later than the males. Gestation lasts from 60 to 75 days, and they give birth to from one to four young ones, usually two. The kittens leave the den at about 28 days. In the field, females are sometimes observed with their offspring, and this is the only time that groups are likely to be seen.

CONSERVATION STATUS

Jaguarundis are placed in CITES Appendix I in Central America and North America. They are considered rare throughout their range. While not exploited specifically for their skins or for the pet trade, they get caught in traps set for other cat species and are often killed because of their predatory raids on domestic animals. As with most other carnivore species, their populations have been deeply hurt by deforestation and habitat destruction. Their extremely large home ranges make them particularly susceptible to habitat encroachment, especially with the consequent negative interactions with humans.

Coatis

Raccoons

and

Relatives

Family
PROCYONIDAE

Coatis, Raccoons,

and Relatives

The procyonids are a diverse and distinct family of carnivores. Mostly omnivores, they have some unusual and interesting species, including the coatis, raccoons, kinkajous, ring-tailed cats, and olingos. With the exception of the lesser panda, a species found only in the Himalayas, they are all from the Americas, thriving in temperate and tropical regions. Most species prefer brushy or forested areas, where they feed on small mammals, amphibians, reptiles, fish, crustaceans, insects, and a variety of fruits and plants. Most species are opportunistic, eating whatever is available at different times of the year.

There are two recognized species of the ring-tailed cat (which, by the way, is not a cat at all), seven species of raccoons (although only two occur in Central America), three species of coatis (one from Central America), three species of olingos (one from Central America), and one species of kinkajou. Raccoons and coatis are the most common and well-known species; ringtails are well known in Mexico and the southern United States, while olingos and kinkajous have been little studied in Central America, leaving their ecological needs, natural history, and conservation status largely unknown.

Raccoons, one of the best-known species, have adapted well to a variety of situations and environments. They thrive in human-impacted environments and have learned to obtain abundant food from people's leftovers. Raccoons have been introduced to other parts of the world, where they seem to have had no problem adapting to the harsh environments of Siberia, Asia, and several European countries. Raccoons have been economically important for many years as a game and fur species, mostly in North America. In Central America, they are seldom hunted for their fur or meat.

Raccoons, coatis, kinkajous, and olingos make intelligent and amusing pets, although a full-grown raccoon or coati is very strong and can be dangerous. Wild individuals are easy to tame and frequently inhabit settled areas. This common practice, however, can lead to uninvited and uncontrollable appearances into kitchens and dining rooms by adults of the species. An adult coati male can destroy a well-stocked kitchen with little effort. Raccoons can also become adept at "breaking and entering," looting, and destroying property.

With the exception of the coatimundis and the olingos, most procyonids are solitary and crepuscular, or active in the twilight. Coatis travel through forested areas in bands composed of females with young and immature males. Most adult male coatis are solitary, moving from band to band at mating time. Olingos regularly travel and forage in trees with kinkajous, although the nature of this relationship is not clear. Most procyonids, particularly the young, are excellent climbers and spend a good portion of their time in trees. The dexterity of raccoons and coatis has generated many stories. It is true that raccoons can manipulate objects with their "hands" and can open doors and windows. However, they do not "wash" their food in streams as it is commonly believed, but rather look for crayfish and other crustaceans under rocks along streams so that it looks as if they are washing their prey when they forage this way.

Procyonids in general have been affected by the accelerated deforestation of Central America. Much of their natural habitat consists of primary and secondary forest, and, with the exception of the raccoon, they do not survive well in clear-cut areas. Even raccoons need brush and trees for building dens and nests and for daytime protection.

WHITE-NOSED COATIMUNDI

(coati) (*Nasua narica*)

The tropical dry forest that once covered much of the Pacific side of Central America—and which has all but disappeared due to the advance of civilization—is home to an incredibly rich and diverse flora and fauna. The six-month dry season that characterizes this forest allows for dramatic changes in the nature of the vegetation. Many trees lose their leaves during the dry season, so the forest looks like a northern winter landscape. Many species of trees also

*Young coati looking out
from behind a tree.*

flower during the leafless months, peppering the landscape with bright splotches of yellow, orange, pink, and red.

While exploring a large patch of dry forest near Cerro El Hacha (Ax Hill) in northern Costa Rica, I encountered a deep ravine with a dry stream at the bottom. I carefully worked my way down into the ravine, clinging to trees and branches, and followed the stream to a large pool. Numerous tracks in the soft mud revealed it was a well-visited watering hole for the local fauna. I continued to follow the dry creek bed upstream. Rounding a bend, I walked into a large group of coatis foraging on the dry forest floor. Panic spread through both coati and human, and a loud and hasty retreat ensued. After recovering my normal vital signs, I walked back to the meeting place and found five little coatis stranded at the top of a tree. I could hear the grunts and calls from the alarmed parents, but could not resist staying for a few minutes to look at these likable creatures.

The little ones clung to the branches, more curious than afraid, emitting soft cries and chirps and climbing one over the other to get a better look at me. Most trees nearby showed scars from climbing adults, evidence of the arboreal habits of this species. However, they mostly forage on the ground, retiring at night to the safety of trees to sleep. Their slightly ringed tails were almost as long as their bodies, and while not prehensile, they probably aid them in keeping their balance while moving around the tree tops.

Concerned at the retreating sounds of the adults, I also backed off, leaving the youngsters free to return to their parents. This was to be the first of many encounters with this common but unique carnivore of tropical forests.

C. DE LA R.

When I first arrived at the field station's main house, there was a cute furry animal sitting on the table on the front porch. It looked tame, and my first reaction was to reach out and pet it, but it immediately snapped at my hand. I was later given all the rules of etiquette around "Nasi," and there were a lot of "don't" rules.

Nasi was a half-tame female coatimundi who had chosen of her own accord to stay around the feline rescue station I was just starting to work in. Several attempts to take her back to the forest near the station had failed. She always found her way back to the station faster than the two-legged creatures that took her for a "walk." She roamed around the house and nearby forest, sometimes leaving for one or two weeks (her "honeymoon" trips, when we would occasionally see her in the forest with her wild mate). As long as one was careful around her, mishaps were few, but there were exceptions.

Once she became accustomed to my presence, she would often come to

me and cuddle on my lap or wrap herself around my neck. This was sometimes a bit painful, for adult coatis are heavy and can be a little rough, even
when they are being nice (unlike cats, they can't retract their claws). One was
wise to learn quickly what not to do, even when she was in her cuddly
moods, because she was fast at using her sharp teeth to correct your misbe-
havior. Nasi had an aversion to keys, coins, nails, or anything that made a jingling sound. She would react with lightning speed, attacking and biting who-
ever was producing the annoying sounds. We hypothesized at length whether
this was a fluke behavior of Nasi's or whether there was an adaptive advantage to having a violent reaction to jingling sounds. However, there are few
sounds in nature that resemble jingling, with perhaps the exception of the
rattle of a rattlesnake. Since then, we have encountered other coatis, including juveniles, with similar reactions to jingling sounds.

Her keen sense of smell also made for interesting antics. She liked anything that smelled nice; she would steal a bar of soap and sit on the roof rub-
bing it on her tail until the soap was completely gone.

Eventually, Nasi was returned to the wild of a nearby forest, where she had
her young. She returned once to the station for a brief visit, but after that
never came back.   C. C. N.

Young coati digging for food.

TAXONOMY AND RELATIVES

Coatimundis, or coatis, are larger and heavier relatives of the raccoon. There are two species of *Nasua* known from the Neotropics. *Nasua narica* is found from southern Arizona and New Mexico to Panama, and *Nasua nasua* is found in South America from Colombia to Argentina. Another species formerly in this genus, *Nasuella olivacea*, is now placed in its own genus and found in the Andes of Venezuela, Colombia, and Ecuador, although it is very rare (Kaufmann, 1983).

There has been some confusion in the past over the taxonomy of this species. Their social behavior prompted early taxonomists to describe two species: a communal species (*Nasua sociabilis*) and a solitary species (*Nasua solitaria*). It was later found that adult males are often solitary, while females with their young and adolescent males stay in groups. The common names of coati (applied to all coatis) and coatimundi (used for the solitary ones) tend to perpetuate this erroneous perception (Kaufmann, 1983).

COMMON NAMES

Coati, coatimundi (English); pizote (Costa Rica); tejón; t'soy (Maya lacandón); zorro guache (Venezuela); tejón, choluga (Mexico); Nasenbär (meaning "nose-bear") (German).

DESCRIPTION

The most striking and notable features of coatis are the long and slightly up-turned nose and the long tail, which is often carried straight up while walking or foraging. Coatis have five toes on each foot and walk like bears, with a plantigrade gait (that is, using the whole sole of the foot). This is typical for procyonids and bears. A running coati reminds one very much of a running grizzly bear.

The white-nosed coati, as the name suggests, possesses a white band around the end of the muzzle. The rest of the muzzle and eye area is dark brown to black. The fur is gray-brown with silver grizzled on the back and arms. They have white throats and bellies, small white spots above and below the eyes, and a bigger one on the cheeks. The feet are black and the tail is noticeably striped. These stripes, while sometimes barely visible from the top, can best be seen on the underside of the tail.

Their size ranges between 80 and 130 cm from head to tail, with the tail being more than half the length of the body. Females weigh between 3.5 and 6 kg, while males weigh between 5 and 8 kg.

Adult female coati feeding.

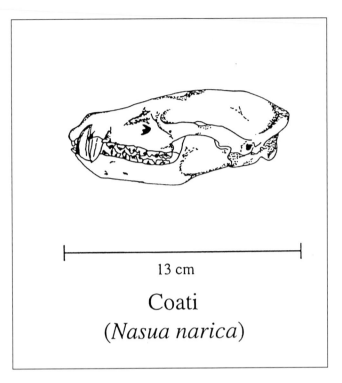

13 cm

Coati
(*Nasua narica*)

DENTAL FORMULA

I3/3, C1/1, P4/4, M2/2, for a total of 40 teeth.

HABITAT AND DISTRIBUTION

Nasua narica can be found from the southwestern United States and Mexico through Central America to Colombia and Ecuador. They live in a variety of different habitats and can be found in dense tropical rain forests, as well as in more temperate scrub lands.

BEHAVIOR

Unlike most of its relatives, the coati is active by day. Their long tails probably serve as balancing aids while in trees. Their main food is comprised of invertebrates that they dig out of the ground or rotting tree trunks. They also like ripe fruits, nuts, small mammals, and frogs, as well as the eggs of birds, turtles, and lizards. They use their long and highly movable noses to sniff and dig for food on the forest floor. Their high cuspid molars and premolars are probably an adaptation to this very insectivorous diet. Coatis

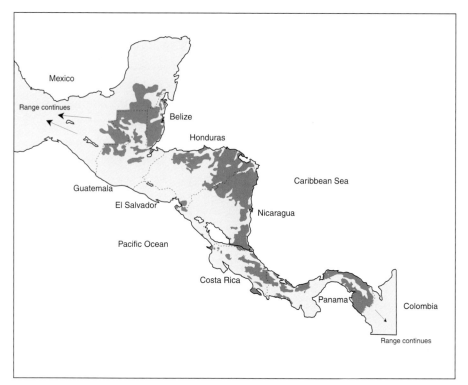

9. *Historical (light) and present (dark) coati distribution.*

can easily dig up roots and other foods from the soil using their long claws
and strong forelimbs. Although juveniles spend a lot of their time in trees,
adults are more terrestrial and forage on the ground. They are also good
climbers.

Male coatis live solitary lives. Outside of the breeding periods, they get
chased away by females because they might harm or kill the juveniles. The
females and young live together in bands. Such bands consist of five to 12 individuals, and the bonds between their members are established and main-
tained by social grooming. Interestingly, the females of a band don't seem to
be related to each other. The bands usually have a home range of about one
kilometer in diameter, but the borders can overlap with other groups that tolerate each other. They have even been seen foraging and grooming together,
which might explain how new groups form by one group dividing into two.

When a predator threatens a band, the young ones are protected by the
adults who charge the predator. Coatis can be very aggressive and fast-moving
when they attack. Their long sharp teeth can cause severe damage. However,
when confronted with big predators or with humans, they usually flee.

Young male coati climbing a tree.

REPRODUCTION

During the breeding season, which can span several months, females become less aggressive towards males. A male, usually the dominant one in the band's range, slowly gains the band members' favor by grooming them. He then mates with the females of the group, usually copulating in a tree.

A female leaves her band between two weeks and a month before the offspring are due, finding a secluded place in a tree to build a nest and to have her young. Because coatis are quite agile with their forepaws, their nests, though at times simple platforms, can also be quite complicated. The animals are very good at improvising and experimenting with different materials. We once observed a female coati building a nest with a rounded ceiling and a higher roof above.

Females have from three to five young, which are blind and not very well developed. At birth they weigh no more than 100 to 200 g and lack their parents' distinct coloring. They are covered with a soft gray fur. The mother returns to the band with the young when they are five to six weeks old. After they return, other females may help with the care for the young and actively participate in their protection. Fathers have been seen joining the group for short periods of time and even join in the grooming of adults and the young. It has been suggested that they are al-

Two stages of nest building.

Baby coati climbing down a tree.

lowed to do so in order to recognize their offspring. Females mature at two years of age, while males usually take three years.

CONSERVATION STATUS

Coatis do not receive any special conservation status, although they have suffered substantial losses of habitat due to deforestation. They are good ambassadors for ecotourism, as they are very interesting and playful. They are relatively common and easy to observe. Coatis don't make good pets. Even though they are very cute and playful, the adults, especially the males, are difficult to control and can cause severe bites. In some agricultural areas near natural forests, coatis raid crops (especially corn) and eat eggs.

NORTHERN RACCOON

(Procyon lotor) and

CRAB-EATING RACCOON

(Procyon cancrivorus)

*Two raccoons
inside a
hollowed log.*

Claudia Nocke '97

The trip so far was uneventful in that there was only one blown tire in the jeep and nobody had gotten hurt. My wife Trish, a friend of hers, and their four kids arrived at Santa Rosa's Naranjo Beach on the North Pacific coast of Costa Rica. The kids scrambled out of the jeep and ran to the beach while Trish and her friend stayed behind to set up camp.

There are two ways to get to Playa Naranjo, which is located deep within Santa Rosa National Park. Either you drive a four-wheel-drive vehicle through the perilous rocky and dusty (in the dry season) trail that drops some 300 meters to the Pacific Ocean, or you walk about 20 kilometers through one of the largest and best-preserved remnants of Pacific dry forests left in Central America. They had chosen to drive. Either way, getting there is the best part of the journey. Along the way you are likely to encounter many representatives of the local fauna. In the dry season, much of the wildlife concentrates around the few small water holes that are left in the area. Sitting quietly in a blind near one of these water holes allows an observer to record many species typical of these forests, such as white-faced capuchin monkeys (*Cebus capucinus*), coatis (*Nasua narica*), raccoons (*Procyon lotor*), white-tailed deer (*Odocoileus virginianus*), agoutis (*Agouti paca*), collared peccaries (*Tayassu tajacu*), and, for those extremely lucky ones, white-lipped peccaries (*Tayassu pecari*) or pumas (*Puma concolor*). Birds, such as the vocal magpie jays; reptiles, such as boa constrictors and anole lizards; and many insects, such as the iridescent blue Morpho butterflies, bees, wasps, grasshoppers, ants, and others, complete the parade.

Normally, most of these animals act nervously around the water holes. There's always the chance of an encounter with a puma; noises made by arriving visitors to the water often send ripples of alarm through whatever group is actually at the hole. Raccoons are not always at the water holes in the upper parts of the trail, but prefer to live and forage closer to the sea shore.

At the camping site, the women unpacked the tent and the food, enough to feed four children and two adults for at least four days. They had heard stories from other campers and residents of the park about raccoons raiding food supplies. Since raccoons live within the protection of a national park, they and other animals become relatively bold in their approach to people. Raccoons were commonly seen at Naranjo Beach searching through the garbage pails, using their dexterous hands to open lids and bypass some of the closing mechanisms the park rangers invented. There was garbage spilled around the pails, mute evidence of the raccoons' previous visit.

They packed the food inside the old Toyota Land Cruiser and joined the children at the beach. There they found remains of turtle eggs dug out of the sand by raccoons and other animals. Hatching turtles, which are common at Naranjo and neighboring Nancite beaches, provide yearly feasts to raccoons, coatis, frigatebirds, and other animals when the eggs get laid, and later when the baby turtles crawl out of their nests and try to make their way to the sea. Raccoons are particularly adept at digging up the fresh nests and feasting on eggs.

At night, the campers had a cold sandwich dinner, packed the food in the cooler inside the car, locked it, and settled to sleep in the tent. Sometime during the night they heard the racket. Things were being thrown around and there was a lot of screaming, grunting, and hissing. The campers figured the raccoons were having their nightly good time at the garbage pails, probably sorting through the meager leftovers of their dinner. However, the racket went on, and it seemed to be coming not from the garbage area, but more from where the car was parked. With a sense of foreboding—and some trepidation—Trish ventured out of the safety of the tent and into the dark night to investigate.

She walked the few dozen meters toward the car and shone a flashlight through the windshield. Two pairs of bright eyes shone back at her from inside the car, and a moment of silence and surprise followed. It didn't last long, though. Both raccoons immediately started to scream and scramble inside the car, looking for the exit which had to be somewhere. She couldn't figure out how had they gotten in, since all doors were closed (and locked) and the windows seemed to be in one piece. Then she saw it: the tiny back window, so small she thought it could not permit a small cat to enter, was open. Somehow the raccoons had squeezed through it and gotten inside, but now couldn't figure out how to get out.

The level of hysteria seemed to be increasing as both raccoons jumped and tore around inside the car, trapped by their own ingenuity. Trish ran back to the tent, got the car keys, and approached the car again. By now both animals were terrified and incredibly loud. She unlocked the driver's side door, opening it quickly and running back away from the car. She didn't see them leave the car, but she heard them run through the brush, still screaming, until silence took over again. By now, the kids and her friend were slowly approaching the car with their flashlights. They could not believe their eyes. There were pieces of food everywhere, mixed in with feces and hair. One of the car seats had a long tear in it, and the stench was overpowering. The cooler was open and its contents gone. The only things salvageable were the cans of tuna fish and vegetables (their skill with their hands only goes so far) and the packs of crackers and cookies they had taken into the tent. For the next two days, they bathed on the beach, washed the car, and ate tuna fish and crack-

Juvenile raccoon sunning on a branch.

ers. As far as the raccoons were concerned, they weren't seen again for the rest of the trip. They didn't miss them much, either.   c. de la r.

TAXONOMY AND RELATIVES

Raccoons belong to the family Procyonidae, but they were first described in 1780 by Linnaeus incredibly under the genus *Ursus* with the bears. They were later placed in their own genus, *Procyon*, by Storr. The scientific name *Procyon* comes from the Latin "pro," meaning before, and "cyon," which means canid. The species name *lotor* also comes from Latin and means "washer," referring to the apparent behavior of washing their food before eating it (which is not actually true). The word "raccoon" comes from the Algonquian (a dialect of the Ojibwa language spoken by some indigenous tribes of the United States) word "arakum," meaning "least like a fox."

There are two species present in Central America: the crab-eating raccoon (*Procyon cancrivorus*), which lives from eastern Costa Rica to Peru and Uruguay, and the northern raccoon (*Procyon lotor*), which lives in North America and Central America into western Panama. Since both species are very similar and closely related, we treat them together in this chapter. They are related to the coatis (*Nasua narica*) and somewhat resemble this species.

Two subgenera have been recognized so far, and four or five other species besides these two have been described for the Americas. Most of the other species are confined to islands in Mexico, the Bahamas, and the Lesser Antilles.

COMMON NAMES

'Coons and ringtails (a misnomer) (United States); mapache, mapachín (Costa Rica); zorro cangrejero (Venezuela); osito lavador (Mexico); tejón (Chihuahua, Mexico); and culú (Yucatán peninsula, Mexico).

DESCRIPTION

Both species of raccoons are very similar in appearance. They both have the conspicuous black "mask" on their faces and clearly visible brown and black rings on their tails. They have broad heads and faces with pointed muzzles, short round ears, and black eyes. *P. lotor*'s fur looks grizzled and thick due to the black tips on the brownish hair and the underfur; *P. cancrivorus* looks thinner and lighter because it lacks this underfur, a probable adaptation to warmer climates. Also, their fur lacks the grizzled effect of *P. lotor*, and the fur on the back of the neck slants forward. *P. lotor*'s body size ranges from 40 to 65 cm, with a tail 25 to 38 cm long. They can weigh from 2.5 to 6.5 kg. On average, males are larger than females. *P. cancrivorus* measures from 54 to 65

Profile of a crab-eating raccoon. Notice the smaller "mask" and short hair.

TABLE 1. *A comparison of the northern raccoon and the crab-eating racoon.*

	Head, body markings, and size	Coloration	Tail	Feet
NORTHERN RACCOON	Generally larger than southern species. Long fur and soft underfur. Grizzled appearance on upper parts of fur, which slants backwards. Animal looks fatter or thicker because of underfur.	Grizzled back and gray upper parts. White face with broad black mask almost to the ears. Brown bars of color on throat. Brown underfur.	About 60% of the length of body. Moderately bushy, with broad brightly contrasting black and gray or buff rings.	Forelegs whitish; hind legs either whitish or brown.
CRAB-EATING RACCOON	Generally smaller than northern species. Neck fur slants backwards toward head. Animal looks thinner because of the lack of underfur.	Less grizzling of the upper parts of fur. Black mask fades behind the eyes.	About 50% the length of the body. Prominent wide black and pale rings.	Legs and feet dark brown and slender looking.

cm in body length, with a tail ranging from 25 to 38 cm, and has a total weight of 3 to 7 kg.

Coloration is relatively variable and one cannot rely on it for positive identification of the species in the field. The extent of the face mask (complete around the eyes in *P. lotor*, incomplete in *P. cancrivorus*), the thinner-looking body of *P. cancrivorus* and the slanting of the fur at the neck (normal in *P. lotor*, "backwards" in *P. cancrivorus*) should aid in proper identification. Both species overlap their ranges in Costa Rica and Panama, which are the countries where confusion of them may occur.

Table 1 provides the main characteristics that differentiate these species.

DENTAL FORMULA

I3/3, C1/1, P4/4, M2/2, for a total of 40 teeth.

HABITAT AND DISTRIBUTION

The northern raccoon lives from southern Canada to the Chiriquí region of Panama. Apparently it is expanding its range further north into Canada as more agricultural area is available. The crab-eating raccoon lives from eastern Costa Rica and Panama south to Uruguay and northeastern Argentina. Both species thrive in a variety of habitats, including primary and secondary forests (generally at low elevations), swamp lands, mangrove forests, beaches, abandoned and cultivated farms, and urban habitats. Apparently, as long as

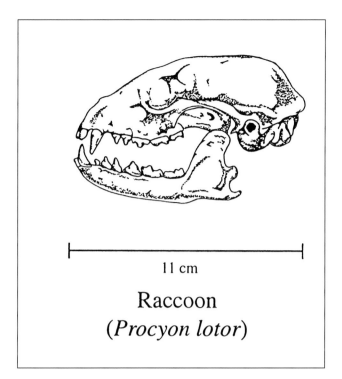

11 cm

Raccoon
(*Procyon lotor*)

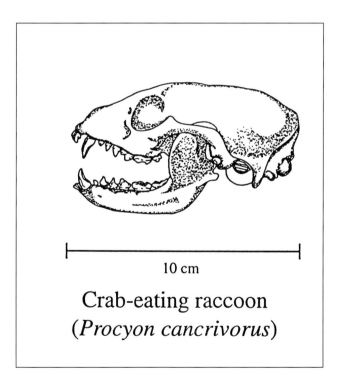

10 cm

Crab-eating raccoon
(*Procyon cancrivorus*)

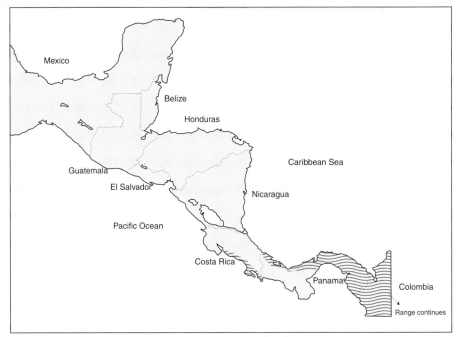

10. *Northern (light) and crab-eating (stripes) raccoon distribution.*

there is water, food (they are omnivorous), and places to hide and den, they will adapt. Because they are highly adaptable, they learn quickly that cities and dumps provide abundant food. Their lack of territoriality allows them to reach very high densities where there are abundant food resources.

The crab-eating raccoon appears more restricted in its habitat preferences, keeping its activities to the areas around water bodies, including rivers, swamps, lakes and lagoons, and ocean beaches. Where both species overlap, crab-eating raccoons tend to occupy inland river habitats, while northern raccoons will live in mangrove swamps and nearby beaches (Emmons, 1997).

BEHAVIOR

Raccoons are normally nocturnal and terrestrial, although both species can climb well, the northern raccoon being more arboreal than the crab-eating raccoon. Both species are omnivorous and eat a wide variety of foods, including invertebrates, crustaceans, insects, fruits, nuts, garden fruits, vegetables, fish, frogs, turtles, and human-produced garbage. Crab-eating raccoons prefer crustaceans, mollusks, fish, amphibians, and insects, balancing their diet with fruits. It is this wide range of food items that allows raccoons to be so successful throughout their range. Their diet changes with the seasons and the availability of food items. In agricultural areas, particularly where corn is planted, rac-

Two adult raccoons playing.

coons can become serious agricultural pests; they eat the new ears of corn and raid chicken coops. Their dexterity is also useful to them in urban areas, where they can open garbage bins and feed on grubs and other insects.

While male raccoons are solitary, they tolerate other raccoons around their feeding areas. Females with young are very social, and the cubs learn all their future skills from the mother. During their first breeding season, young males will disperse to other areas, while young females tend to remain near the range of their mothers. Raccoons live for about five years in the wild, although captive individuals can live for up to 20 years.

Raccoons have many predators in nature, and they are particularly attractive to pumas, coyotes, foxes, and feral dogs. But the major predators of raccoons are humans. Humans are also responsible for many road-related deaths, as well as deaths related to domestic animal diseases such as rabies and canine distemper.

Something should be said about the alleged "washing of the food" behavior observed in many captive and wild raccoons. Raccoons are very dexterous and are adept at manipulating small items. They are commonly observed dipping their hands in the water (rivers, streams, or ponds) and "washing" their food before eating it. It is widely accepted now that this behavior is innate,

Raccoon cleaning.

more related to foraging for aquatic prey such as crayfish than to "cleanliness." Captive raccoons will often "wash" their food outside of the water!

REPRODUCTION

Raccoons breed once a year, with strong seasonal tendencies in northern latitudes. In Central America, they tend to breed around the beginning of the rainy season (from November on), but there is much variation reported, with breeding occurring almost any time during the year. *P. cancrivorus* appears to breed between July and September in southern latitudes.

Male raccoons are polygamous, mating with several females in succession; females, on the other hand, reject all males once they have been impregnated. Females mature sexually during their first year, while males, although sexually capable of mating, usually cannot compete with larger, more mature males during their first year. Mating events can be extremely noisy and disturbing for the neighbors. Males will fight each other for access to females, and they are very vocal about it. Gestation periods last between 60 and 75 days, resulting in the birth of two to four young.

Dens consist of hollow trees, rock crevices, culverts, abandoned buildings, wood or brush piles, and other animals' dens adapted to their needs. Raccoon cubs are very small and helpless, born without teeth and with their eyes closed. After two weeks their eyes open, and they begin to show the characteristic mask on their faces. Weaning occurs at about two months, but they begin foraging with the female a few weeks before that. The two species do not appear to interbreed in areas where they overlap.

Baby raccoon peering out of nest.

CONSERVATION STATUS

Raccoons have, through much of their northern range, an important economic impact, both positive and negative. *P. lotor* is one of the most important fur species in the United States, although the demand for its pelts has been decreasing. Raccoons were formerly prized as pets, because of their intelligence and manual abilities. They are easily tamed and may adapt quickly to a wilder mode of life once they are grown and mature sexually. However, like coatis, they become unmanageable as they mature; adult raccoons make very poor pets. Also, due to their propensity to carry diseases such as rabies, leptospirosis, tularemia, and others, caution should be observed when interacting with wild raccoons or when inspecting their feces.

Raccoons are considered pests in some agricultural and many urban areas, as well as in wildlife management areas where the interest lies in waterfowl. Raccoons often destroy duck nests and eat the eggs and ducklings. Control measures are generally inefficient and often increase some of the problems associated with the spread of disease.

In northern ranges, the raccoon is managed as a game species through hunting and trapping. There is no management program in Central America. While no protection is given to raccoons throughout much of their southern range, *P. cancrivorus* probably should have it. While less common than *P. lotor* in Central America, this species appears to be doing well in the wild.

KINKAJOU

(Potos flavus)

The rainy morning gave a little chill to the atmosphere of PROFELIS, the wild cat rescue center where I had just started working as a volunteer assistant to the station's researchers. At that time, the center was located in a small part of a cattle ranch surrounded by patches of forests, in an area between the Miravalles and Tenorio volcanoes in northern Costa Rica. Las Flores, the nearest community, boasted about 200 inhabitants, mostly farmers and ranch hands. The climate around Las Flores was predominantly wet. People in the area joked that it rained 13 months a year in Las Flores, and this was not far from the truth. In such a humid and wet area, mold grew on everything that stayed motionless for more than a day.

On my first morning at the station I was shown around and introduced to its inhabitants. The first few days of work were filled with surprises and ex-

Portrait of
a male
kinkajou
on a tree.

citement, and every new cage I visited usually held some unexpected wonder. Although it was a wild cat center, PROFELIS had some nonfeline guests living at the station. This was a result of many animals who were illegally kept as pets being confiscated by the Wildlife Department and there being too few adequate places to take them. In one cage close to the house was a spider monkey (*Ateles geoffroyi*) who had spent 19 years of his life chained to a tree. Now, at least, he enjoyed the relative freedom of a large cage.

The next cage was a small, funny-looking A-frame structure that I had not noticed before, located next to a large roofed cage that housed rabbits and quail, which were raised as food for the cats. I opened the door of the A-frame and quietly stepped inside, wary of what I might find there. There was no animal in sight, and no sound came from the square wooden box whose entrance was covered by a small towel. These boxes usually served as sleeping quarters for the animal guests; I slowly lifted the little towel and peered inside. Two sleepy eyes looked back at me, an unwelcome intruder who was waking it up at this time of "night": it was early morning, but for this young male kinkajou it was time to sleep.

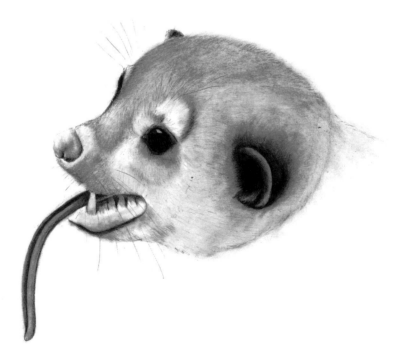

Kinkajou showing his very long tongue.

As I found out later, "Wickler" was our resident kinkajou. They are also known as "honey bears" because of reports of them feeding on the honey of wild bees. Wickler had been outside the cage roaming in the trees all night and was now quite tired. A big yawn showed at least 20 centimeters of flattened tongue. It was so long that I wondered how in the world it could fit into such a small mouth. He also had a wealth of small but sharp teeth. In later days, once little Wickler got used to me, I found this tongue investigating every thing it could find. Not even my ears were spared. I also noticed a sweet, warm smell on Wickler which reminded me a bit of the smell of fresh pancakes when he wrapped himself around my neck.

As with many other kinkajous, Wickler had been captured when very young, tamed, and kept as a pet by a farmer's family near the center. However, even in captivity, kinkajous retain their nocturnal habits, which do not match well the diurnal habits of humans. Tired of the nightly shenanigans of their pet, they had donated him to the station.

Kinkajous have very dexterous front paws. Nighttimes were filled with excitement when Wickler, who was free to roam and forage in the trees surrounding the station at night, would find his way inside the station house by ripping off the window screens or wooden panels under the roof. He then would noisily roam the house looking for food and other things of interest. If not stopped in time, he would leave a scene of total disorder, particularly in the bathroom! He would also drop from the ceiling or from the window sills onto the beds of the sleeping inhabitants. Believe me, it is quite an experience to be awakened by a kinkajou jumping on your head in the middle of the dark night!

Every morning at dawn Wickler returned to his open cage and spent the day sleeping. He woke up for a "midnight snack" around noon, and quickly returned to his tightly scheduled rest.   C. C. N.

TAXONOMY AND RELATIVES

The kinkajou, *Potus flavus*, was first described by Schreber in 1774, although under a completely different genus (*Viverra*, which itself was a synonym for *Lemur*). Their closest relatives in Central America are the olingos (*Bassaricyon gabbii*), cacomistles (*Bassariscus sumichrasti*), raccoons (*Procyon* spp.) and coatis (*Nasua narica*).

COMMON NAMES

Kinkajou, honey bear (United States); kinkajú (Spanish); cuchicuchi (Venezuela); martilla (Costa Rica); mico de noche (Nicaragua); micoleón (Honduras);

marta, martucha, tancho, oso mielero, godoy (Mexico); Wickelbär (meaning "bear that wraps around") (German).

DESCRIPTION

The kinkajou possesses one unique feature for a New World carnivore: a prehensile tail. Kinkajous may look a bit like monkeys and, in fact, for a while they were classified with the lemurs. Kinkajous can be easily confused with olingos (*Bassaricyon gabbii*), but the kinkajou tail, besides being prehensile, is shorter than its head-body length and is of one color, short-haired, and slightly tapering. The bodies of kinkajous are stockier, and they lack one premolar and anal sacs. There are bare patches near the corner of the kinkajou's mouth. On the throat and belly are scent glands that produce a pleasant, sweet musky smell. The soft, woolly fur is brown or gray with a honey-colored underside. The head is round and small compared to the elongated body. It has a fairly short, blunt muzzle, small, round ears, and dark, round eyes. The mouth is quite small, but when the kinkajou sticks out its thin tongue, you are in for a surprise: the tongue measures around 20 cm, and it is highly extendible.

Their hind legs are longer than their front ones and can rotate 180 degrees at the ankles. This allows them to hang from their hind legs from a branch, clinging to it with the sharp claws of the hind feet. Unlike cats, kinkajous cannot retract their claws. At 2 to 4 kg in weight, kinkajous are approximately the size of domestic cats. Unlike cats, kinkajous walk on the whole foot, not just on the toes. The underside of the kinkajous' feet is leathery and bare-skinned, and the inside of their front paws looks remarkably like our hands. These front paws are very dexterous and kinkajous use them in captivity to open enclosures by undoing hooks or other locking devices. The head-body length of the kinkajou is about 45 to 75 cm, males being larger than the females.

Table 2 should help differentiate the four most-often confused species (data mostly from Emmons, 1997, and Eisenberg, 1989).

DENTAL FORMULA

I3/3, C1/1, P3/3, M2/2, for a total of 36 teeth.

HABITAT AND DISTRIBUTION

Kinkajous are found from southern Mexico to southern Brazil, usually at elevations ranging from sea level to about 500 meters, although they have been reported as high as 1,750 meters (Emmons, 1997). They require some forest

TABLE 2. *A comparison of cacomistles, olingos, kinkajous, and coatimundis.*

	Head, body markings, and size	Coloration	Tail	Claws	Other distinguishing characteristics
CACOMISTLE	Small and slender, with a relatively long neck and small head. Very large ears.	Tawny brown with a blackish line on back. Dirty yellow to whitish rings around the eyes. Yellowish-white underparts.	Ringed, longer than head and body, thickly furred, nonprehensile.	Long, curved, semiretractile on front paws.	Solitary, almost exclusively arboreal.
OLINGO	Slender body, short legs, and "monkeylike" appearance and movement. Smaller than kinkajou.	Brown, often darker in midline. Crown often dark brown. Underparts cream.	Lightly ringed, slightly longer than head and body, nonprehensile.	Nonretractile.	Nocturnal, arboreal, solitary.
KINKAJOU	Agile, "monkeylike" appearance and movement. Muscular and short-legged. Rounder face than olingo or cacomistle.	Reddish brown or grayish brown, often with a darker ridge band, short and dense fur. Underparts yellow to orange buff.	Not ringed, slightly longer than head and body, prehensile, tapered toward tip.	Long, curved claws, nonretractile.	Ears small and round, set low on the sides of the head. Very long and agile tongue. Nocturnal canopy animal.
COATIMUNDI	Largest species in table. Looks like a tall, slender raccoon without the black mask.	Dark brown, with grayish shoulders. White nose, which is long and mobile. Muzzle and chin white.	Ringed (although can be inconspicuously ringed in some populations), shorter than body, nonprehensile.	Long and curved, nonretractile.	Mostly terrestrial habits, although young and some adults do climb trees. Forage in family groups.

cover in order to thrive, preferring to stay within the canopy of primary and secondary forests. Their omnivorous diet, strongly based on fruits (they are also known to feed on nectar), requires the year-round variety that mature forest types provide. They also visit plantations, gardens, gallery forests, and deciduous forests (Emmons, 1997).

BEHAVIOR

The kinkajou is nocturnal and spends its days resting on branches or sleeping in secluded places such as tree holes. Being highly arboreal, it rarely leaves the canopy. As a frugivore (fruit-eater)/omnivore, the kinkajou also likes small vertebrates, insects, frogs' eggs, leaves, bark, and honey, in addition to

Young male kinkajou climbing. Notice prehensile tail.

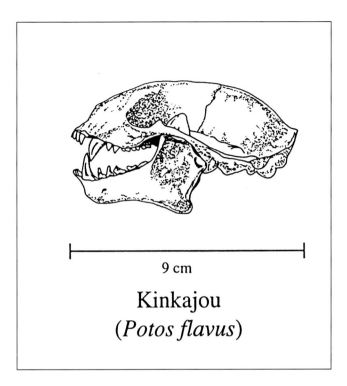

9 cm

Kinkajou
(*Potos flavus*)

11. *Historical (light) and present (dark) kinkajou distribution.*

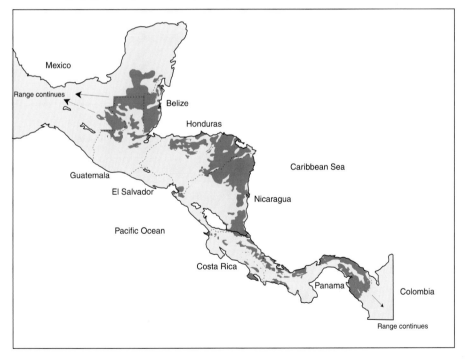

Portrait of young kinkajou.

Claudia Nocke '98

the fruits that comprise a big portion of its diet. Sometimes they even manage to catch small roosting birds. They rarely touch citrus or acidy fruits, while any fruit that is sweet is eaten with relish. When eating soft, juicy fruits, the kinkajou often lies on its back, in order to catch even the juice of the fruit. One study (Charles-Dominique et al., 1981) reported kinkajous to be good seed dispersers for figs and other species, because seeds pass intact through the kinkajou's gut. Their long tongues can easily be used to extract pollen and nectar from tree blossoms. They can be very fast and move mainly in the tree tops.

Kinkajous often move alone or in pairs, but have been observed to form small temporary groups in fruit-laden trees. Although individuals use scent-marking to define their territories and travel routes, they don't appear to defend territories. Shrill chirp/whistle vocalizations can be heard from the branches above where kinkajous are feeding. Apparently, they use high-pitched sounds for calling short distances, barks for medium-range contacts, and shrill screams for long distances. These screams can be heard for up to one-and-a-half kilometers. When threatened, kinkajous make a barklike sound. Finally, observing kinkajous from underneath a feeding tree can often lead to fruity-sweet scat "accidents."

Natural enemies of kinkajous are margays, ocelots, jaguarundis, gray foxes, and tayras.

REPRODUCTION

There seems to be no distinct breeding season for the kinkajou. After a gestation period of 98 to 118 days, usually one young is born. Twins are rare, and more than two young could probably not survive, as the females have only two mammae on the lower abdomen. The young are usually born in tree holes and at birth weigh as little as 150 g. Within two or three weeks they start opening their eyes; after their third to sixth month the tail becomes prehensile. The young start foraging with the mother, feeding on solid food to supplement the milk. They stay with the mother for a minimum of six months. While males reach maturity at 18 months, females can take more than two years. Pairs can stay together for many years and in captivity they can live up to 23 years.

In mating observed in captive pairs, it appears that secretions from scent glands play a role in initiation of mating behaviors. The male rubs the sides of the female to stimulate her, using an enlarged portion of the wrist bone on the inside of his wrists. The bone is also present in the female, but it is covered with fur and not noticeable. After the female has been thus stimulated, copulation occurs. Although there are many kinkajous in zoos and private collections, they do not often breed in captivity.

CONSERVATION STATUS

Kinkajous, as other inhabitants of primary and secondary forests, have suffered from the rapid rate of deforestation of the isthmus. They do little damage to cultivated fruits and fruit plantations, so they are not normally persecuted for being pests, although in some parts of their range they are hunted for their meat and fur. They are listed in CITES Appendix III (in Honduras), but probably require some attention in other countries as well.

The observations on mating described here were carried out by personnel of the Carnivore Preservation Trust, a nonprofit organization dedicated to the protection and preservation of world carnivores. They hold the largest captive population of kinkajous and have been successful in breeding them.

OLINGO

(Bassaricyon gabbii)

*Olingo looking
down from a tree.*

The lowland rain forest of the Indio-Maíz Biological Reserve, on the southeastern corner of Nicaragua, constitutes one of the largest relatively undisturbed patches of natural forest left in Central America. The almost 300,000 hectare reserve is joined on the south by Tortuguero National Park and the Barra del Colorado Wildlife Refuge in Costa Rica. It forms one of the largest uninterrupted patches of protected ecosystems in the region. This protection is, however, tenuous at best, because there is little infrastructure and almost no personnel to protect or manage such a vast area. As part of an Organization of American States' study in the San Juan River Basin, we were traveling the length of the San Juan River between Costa Rica and Nicaragua, investigating the state of the biodiversity resources of the watershed. The intention was to provide an assessment and guidelines for preliminary conservation actions.

For two days we traveled on a flat and noisy diesel-powered boat that was crowded with farmers and settlers on their way to some very remote farms and villages. Claudia, Rigoberto, and I finally arrived at the small town of San Juan del Norte at the mouth of the San Juan River. After getting settled in the only small and rustic lodge in town, we arranged for a night boat trip along some smaller tributaries of the river. According to our maps, these were deep inside the undisturbed forests. Boats are the main form of transportation in a place where there are no roads at all, and the rivers and tributaries provide a vast and often unexplored highway network. We started the trip shortly before sunset on an open motor boat owned by Ricardo, the brother of the lodge owner. Ricardo knew the river well; it had been his neighborhood and playground when he was a child. The river provided a new source of income for his family in recent months as he began taking tourists and biologists like us into the area. It also served as a supermarket where he could get fish and meat for the table, so he knew where to look for animals. Our mission was to get an idea of how disturbed this apparently pristine area was and determine the relative density of the local fauna. Ricardo's running commentary and anecdotes would also provide some additional information.

Ricardo wove his way into a tributary of the larger Maíz River, which was a place frequented by manatees. Night was setting in and our strong flashlights scanned the close green wall that went uninterrupted on both sides of the river.

"There!" said Claudia, pointing at a group of monkeylike animals in the canopy of a fruit-laden fig tree. Ricardo stopped the motor, and we drifted slowly toward the edge of the forest. We focused our binoculars on the group while Ricardo pointed the light beams at the blinking creatures.

"They are kinkajous," I said. "A whole bunch of them."

Face of an adult olingo.

"No they're not!" Claudia said. "They are something else. Wait."

I followed the one I was looking at, losing it now and then as Ricardo switched the lights from one animal to another. The bright shine of their eyes in the light was distracting, and I couldn't see all the details I wanted to see.

"Are you sure?" I asked. "Mine looks just like Wickler," I continued; Wickler was the resident kinkajou at the cat rescue station Claudia had worked at in the past.

"I worked with Wickler, Carlos, and this thing is not a kinkajou," she responded. She had her own flashlight back and was following one of the animals as it slowly moved from branch to branch.

"Are you sure we're looking at the same thing?" I asked, "because if this is not a kinkajou, I have to go back to school! Ricardo, what do you call these things?"

I took my flashlight from Ricardo and shone it at one of the animals.

"A martilla!" he said without a doubt, which was the local common name for the kinkajou.

"See? I was right," I said. Meanwhile, Claudia was silent, looking at the kinkajou I had under my light and switching to the one she was following with the other light.

"There's something strange here," she said. "These are not the same species. I think one of them is an olingo. Look at the striped tail on that one."

I did look, and while very light, there seemed to be faint stripes on the tail on one. Also, the kinkajous were grabbing branches with their prehensile tails, but the other's tail seem to be thicker and just hanging, not grabbing things.

Back at the hotel, we looked at our field guides and decided that we had seen a group of kinkajous and an olingo together, something that we later found out was not an uncommon event. Ricardo, looking at both pictures in Emmons's field guide, decided that he had seen both of them at one time or another, but that he didn't know they were different. He just called them all "martillas." C. DE LA R.

TAXONOMY AND RELATIVES

Of the five species of olingos presently recognized, *B. gabbii* is the most common one. *B. pauli* and *B. lasius* are only known from their type localities (the places where the specimens used to describe the species originally came from) in western Panama and central Costa Rica respectively. The genus was first proposed by J. A. Allen in 1876, who described *B. gabbii* from Costa Rica. There are two other species in South America. Some sources (Emmons, 1997; Reid, 1997) suggest that all of these species are probably the same (*B. gabbii*).

COMMON NAMES

Olingo (English); martilla (a misnomer in Costa Rica). Because they are not very well known and are often confused with kinkajous, people use the same common names for the olingo and the kinkajou.

DESCRIPTION

The first impression of an olingo is that it is very similar to a kinkajou or a cacomistle. It is slightly smaller than the kinkajou and more slender, though not as delicate, as the cacomistle. As in the kinkajou, the olingo has a slightly monkeylike face with a round head, big, round eyes, and round, forward-pointing ears, though the muzzle in the gray grizzled face is slightly longer and more pointed. It has a soft, dense fur that is a muddy brown color above and lighter on the undersides. The crown and occasionally the midline of the

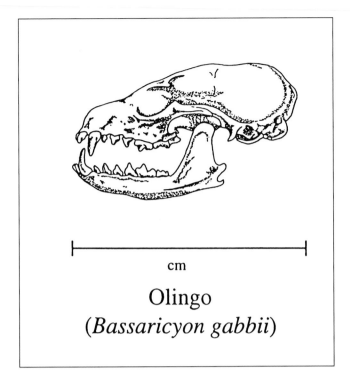

cm

Olingo
(*Bassaricyon gabbii*)

back is darker. Kinkajous and olingos both have long bodies and a very short-legged appearance. The tail of the olingo is slightly longer than its head-body length of 35 to 48 cm. It is nonprehensile and covered with long plush fur that may display subtle ring markings. Unlike the tail of the kinkajou, the tail of the olingo looks slightly larger at its tip. In contrast, the cacomistle has pale to white rings around the eyes, larger ears, and a strongly striped tail, with the last quarter being very dark to black; their claws are also nonretractile.

DENTAL FORMULA
I3/3, C1/1, P4/4, M2/2, for a total of 40 teeth.

HABITAT AND DISTRIBUTION
Olingos are found in rain forests from Nicaragua to northern Ecuador and Bolivia. They appear restricted to undisturbed or slightly disturbed primary forests below 2,000 meters. They live and feed in the upper canopy. They are less common than kinkajous but are occasionally seen feeding and moving through the trees with them.

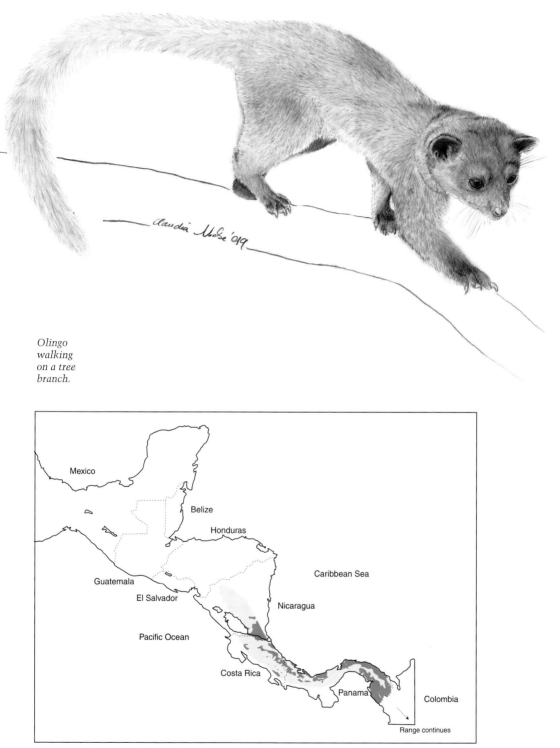

Olingo walking on a tree branch.

12. *Historical (light) and present (dark) olingo distribution.*

BEHAVIOR

Olingos are nocturnal hunters and almost exclusively arboreal. Very good and agile climbers, they are able to jump up to three meters and move swiftly from branch to branch while feeding. Their main foods are ripe fruits, small invertebrates, nuts, and nectar from flowers of trees such as balsa. Olingos can be found foraging together with kinkajous, which offers good opportunities to see the differences between them. They are not considered to be good flower pollinators like the kinkajous. During the day they sleep and rest in nests built in tree holes. They are solitary animals but sometimes move in pairs. They can also be found foraging with opossums (*Didelphis marsupialis*) or night monkeys (*Aotus* spp.) (Emmons, 1997). Males have been seen scent-marking with urine. The function of this, however, is not quite clear as they don't defend territories.

REPRODUCTION

Females have a single pair of mammae, and they normally have one young at a time. Apparently, the only data on reproductive behavior was recorded in captivity at the Louisville Zoo (Poglyen-Neuwall, 1966), where four births resulted in one young each. The gestation period was between 73 and 74 days. The young seemed to be very slow developers, opening their eyes at around 27 days and only taking solid food at eight weeks of age. They became sexually mature in just under two years. In captivity they can live 17 years or more.

CONSERVATION STATUS

Olingos are listed under CITES Appendix III in Costa Rica, but apparently they are not protected anywhere else in Central America. Given their preference for primary rain forests, they are probably more threatened than we think, and their distribution and abundance have been reduced. They are not hunted or harvested for meat or fur.

CACOMISTLE

(Bassariscus sumichrasti) and

RING-TAILED CAT

(Bassariscus astutus)

Portraits of a ring-tailed cat (above) and a cacomistle (below).

Seeing a cacomistle for the first time can be a confusing event. First you see the tail, which has a sequence of dark and light rings, and you think, "Ah! A coatimundi." But no, there is something different about its shape and the way it moves. You look at the whole animal, and yes, there is something odd about it: smaller and more slender than a coatimundi, it has a rounder, more juvenile-looking face and a long ringed tail almost as long as its body. The caco-mistle can climb straight up a tree in one fluid motion, whereas adult coatis are not as agile in climbing. Then, perhaps, you might think it is a kinkajou; kinka-jous are better known and relatively common in wet forests throughout

Ring-tailed cat resting on a tree.

the area, but they have unmarked prehensile tails which are not ringed. In contrast, cacomistle tails are ringed but not prehensile. Cacomistles and ring-tailed cats are not particularly common in Central America. The cacomistle appears to prefer more humid environments than the more northern ring-tailed cat. In forested areas of Central America, both species are relatively rare and seldom seen. C. DE LA R.

TAXONOMY AND RELATIVES

There are two species of cacomistle in the region: the ring-tailed cat (*Bassariscus astutus*), which extends its range into the southern United States (and about which there is abundant information in published research), and *B. sumichrasti*, the less common Central American cacomistle. Neither of them is a cat nor are they related to the felids (except at the higher level of Carnivora). They are more closely related to olingos (*Bassaricyon gabbii*) and kinkajous (*Potos flavus*), which they resemble, raccoons (*Procyon* spp.), and coatimundis (*Nasua narica*).

The genus *Bassariscus* was first described by Coues in 1887, from specimens found in Mexico. *B. sumichrasti* was formerly placed in a separate genus (*Jentinkia*), but this is no longer valid.

COMMON NAMES

Cacomistle, ring-tailed cat (English); bassarise, guayanoche (Guatemala); guía de león, gato de monte, rintel, uayuc (Honduras); caco-mixtle, mico de noche, sal coyote, pinto-rabo (Mexico).

DESCRIPTION

Slender and long, the body of a cacomistle can measure from 30 to 47 cm in length, with a tail length of around 40 to 54 cm. They can weigh from 300 to 400 g to up to 900 g (Emmons, 1997; Nowak, 1991). The characteristic long tail (longer than its body) is clearly ringed, with the rings becoming diffused toward the dark or black tip. The fur is soft, smooth, and grayish-brown in color. The body is darker on top and whitish to light tan underneath. They also have a whitish rim around the eyes which makes them distinct from olingos or kinkajous. The ears are pointed and fairly large for the size of the head. They have long nonretractable claws, a possible adaptation to a more arboreal life style. They are reported to be nocturnal, using tree cavities or hollow stumps as resting places. They seldom come down from the trees, which is another reason why they are seldom seen.

DENTAL FORMULA

I3/3, C1/1, P4/4, M2/2, for a total of 40 teeth.

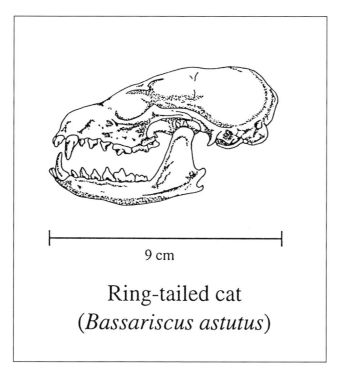

9 cm

Ring-tailed cat
(*Bassariscus astutus*)

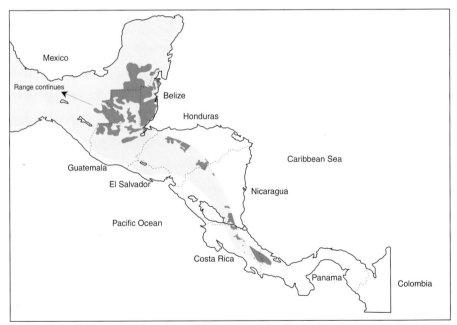

Cacomistle on a tree branch.

HABITAT AND DISTRIBUTION

Cacomistles are found in the mid to high portions of primary or secondary humid forests, at elevations from sea level to about 2,000 meters. They are reported from southern Mexico to eastern Panama, near the border with Costa Rica, although they are rare throughout their range.

BEHAVIOR

Cacomistles are opportunistic omnivorous mammals. They feed on small vertebrates, insects, and fruits they collect from the canopy. They have been reported to eat tree squirrels, birds and eggs, lizards, mice, rats, and occasionally domestic fowl.

Mexico

Range continues

Belize

Honduras

Caribbean Sea

Guatemala

El Salvador

Nicaragua

Pacific Ocean

Costa Rica

Panama

Colombia

13. *Historical (light) and present (dark) ring-tailed cat and cacomistle distribution.*

They seem to be solitary, emitting short barks and a long, loud, high-pitched call that may serve a territorial function (Eisenberg, 1989, and references therein). Their eyes shine bright yellow to white when illuminated.

The Central American species has been little studied. Its habitat is so unlike that of its better-studied northern relative (the ring-tailed cat, which lives in arid and semi-arid lands in northern Mexico and the southern United States) that we hesitate to make too many extrapolations from those studies.

REPRODUCTION

Normally solitary, cacomistles form more or less stable pairs during the breeding season. Captive pairs were observed to jointly care for the young. Although little is known about their mating and reproductive habits, they are assumed to be similar to those of *B. astutus*, which have from one to four young after an approximately 54-day gestation period. They apparently breed year-round, although late winter appears to be the main breeding season (Nowak, 1991, and references therein). Most studies of reproduction in this species were done with captive animals.

CONSERVATION STATUS

In the earlier part of the century, cacomistles (both species) were hunted for their skins, although

Ring-tailed cat climbing a tree.

they never produced very high quality furs. Also, they were often welcome visitors to barns and grain silos where they would control rodent populations. They were less welcome around chicken coops. If captured young, they could be domesticated and apparently made good pets. However, in more recent times, there has been very little interest in and research on these species, and their rarity might be hiding an unknown level of sensitivity to disturbance or habitat reduction. They are listed under CITES Appendix III in Costa Rica, but most other countries offer no protection to cacomistles.

Ring-tailed cat feeding on a moth.

Skunks

Grisons

Weasels

Otters

and

Others

Family
MUSTELIDAE

Skunks, Grisons, and Others

Weasels, Otters,

Of all the carnivore families of Central America, mustelids are perhaps the most diverse and interesting as far as adaptations, habits, and habitats are concerned. The members of this family share a unique characteristic from which the name of the family originated: they all have a pair of glands at the base of the tail on each side of the anus from which they excrete a strongly odorous substance, the musk. In skunks, these glands are greatly developed and serve as defensive weapons. Anyone who has been the target of an angry or scared skunk can attest to the power of musk. In otters, grisons, and weasels, the musk is emitted at times of excitement or fear, but it is not as powerful or effective as it is in skunks.

Most mustelids are predators of small mammals, including rodents and squirrels, but also prey on birds, insects, and amphibians. They can be fierce predators, and they consume great amounts of food for their size. Weasels, for example, kill their prey (mostly birds and small rodents) with uncanny efficiency. Some of them have food caches where they store the uneaten spoils of their hunting forays. The majority of terrestrial mustelids depend on their keen sense of smell to hunt; they have a good sense of hearing but relatively poor sight. Otters depend on their well-developed sense of touch, particularly on the whiskers, which they use as a guidance system to move through the water and hunt aquatic organisms like fish and crustaceans. The majority of the species have diurnal habits, although some skunks and weasels hunt successfully at night.

In Central America, mustelids breed during the entire year, with variations and patterns adjusted to particular microclimatic regions. They generally have one or two litters per year. Some species have "delayed implantation" in which the fertilized embryo doesn't start to grow until months have elapsed. This gives some species extremely long gestation periods of up to a year in some cases. Litter sizes vary from one or two up to ten, with three to five being the norm. Young stay with their mothers for several months and generally disperse during the first year of their life. Most groups of mustelids found in nature consist of a mother and her young. Otherwise, mustelids tend to live solitary lives.

Mustelids can be found in many habitats and life zones in Central America, concentrating in brushy or forested areas. Otters are aquatic and live in rivers and connected lagoons. The skunks and weasels have learned to share their habitat with humans and even thrive on their activities. Weasels are known to attack chickens, and skunks like to raid garbage pits. Skunks can be easily tamed and become used to humans who feed them, although skunks and weasels are seldom kept as pets.

Central American mustelids are represented by one species of weasel, one otter, the tayra, the grison, and three species of skunks. There are several subspecies that have been recognized in some of these groups, and these are distributed in specific areas of the species' ranges. Often, these subspecific populations are not in contact with each other, but isolated in pockets of habitats throughout the species' ranges.

The species of this family produce what are considered some of the finest pelts; among the most valuable are mink, short-tailed weasel (also known as the ermine), and sable, a name which refers to several species of the genus *Martes*. However, Central American mustelids, perhaps with the exception of the river otter and the long-tailed weasel, have not been pursued heavily for their fur, although hunting and trapping of most of the species is allowed throughout most of the isthmus. Over much of their northern range, hunting and trapping is a common wildlife management tool. While mink farms or ranches are common in the United States and produce millions of dollars' worth of pelts every year, there are few commercial operations in Central America. Skunks are a primary vector of rabies in some regions of the United States, although there have been few studies in Central America. They are not kept as pets or harvested for their fur in Central America or the United States.

Mustelids, as most carnivores, play an important ecological role wherever they live. Farmers in many parts of Central America have learned that skunks and weasels are good natural rodent controls and that their presence should be encouraged, chicken-coop raids notwithstanding. These can be avoided by keeping the poultry pens well-protected by wire fences. Some mustelids can be trained to perform certain services to humans. Grisons and ferrets, for example, have been taught to go into rabbit and rodent burrows in order to flush them out; river otters have been trained in China to help their owners fish.

*Portrait of a
tayra chewing
on a branch.*

TAYRA
(Eira barbara)

It was about 3 P.M. on a sunny day in August. Sigi and Sabine were out check-
ing the old river bed near the PROFELIS wildcat rescue station. Two weeks
earlier, on July 27, the station had been devastated by the passage of hurricane Caesar through Costa Rica and Nicaragua. That fateful night a new river
bed was carved through the forest above the station by the intense rains. The
torrents broke through the forest, bringing down huge trees and carrying tons
of mud, rock, and debris with them. The ensuing mud flood destroyed many
of the cat cages and cut off the staff from communications, supplies, and electricity. Now, weeks later, the two biologists were surveying the damage on
the upper watershed and in the old river bed, finding it hard to believe just
how wild and dangerous this little river could become with an unusually high
rainfall.

Sigi walked a few meters in front of Sabine, gingerly picking his way
among the rocks. Out of the corner of her eye, Sabine suddenly saw what reg-
istered as "a small black cat" running on the bank of the river. She shouted to
Sigi, who turned around quickly but couldn't see anything. She hadn't been
able to see it very clearly, as it was all over too quickly, but it had moved like
one of their ocelots. Not wanting to miss the rare opportunity to see a melanistic (black-colored) ocelot or margay, Sigi ran to where he thought the animal would probably reappear, trying to cut off its path so he could observe it.

A few minutes later a large black male tayra nearly ran into him. It came
to an abrupt stop not two meters from where Sigi stood. It turned around and
raced back the way it came. Meanwhile, Sabine was looking for some tracks
where she had seen the "black cat." The tayra, still running away from where
it had met Sigi, now nearly bumped into her and quickly took off in another
direction. Sabine was stunned to see that the "black cat" had turned out to be
a tayra. She always said that she just didn't know how some people could
mistake a tayra for a cat. They had a tayra in their cat station along with over
40 cats. She knew that when you look at them closely it becomes obvious
that tayras are not cats, but if you only see them out of the corner of your
eye, moving very fast, it is a different matter. After their encounter with the
tayra, it became clear why people often confuse this handsome animal with
its relatives, the cats.   C. C. N.

Out of the corner of my eye I saw the black form leap from the bushes on the
side of the road and streak in front of the car. My reflexes took over and I
stepped hard on the brakes. The tires screeched as I tried to avoid running
over an animal that was disappearing under the car. Michelle, my assistant,
screamed in the seat next to me, and I heard a muffled thump on the right

side of the car. I regained control of the careening vehicle and stopped by the side of the road.

"What was that?" Michelle asked.

"I think I hit it, whatever it was," I said. I turned on the emergency lights and left the car to look at the animal.

Traveling on a recently paved road between the Miravalles and Tenorio volcanoes in northern Costa Rica, we were on our way to a meeting in a nearby city. I was dressed in city clothes and was driving a brand-new rental car I had picked up a few days before. My own beat-up four-wheel-drive vehicle was in the shop for repairs. Often during my drives in the countryside I would stop and pick up road kills that I could add to our study collections. Over the years, I had accumulated a wide assortment of skulls, skins, and skeletons that were used in research or education programs. In my own car I always kept a supply of plastic bags, gloves, a machete, and a large cooler where I could keep specimens until my return to the laboratory. I also carried a first-aid kit to aid humans and nonhumans alike. Today I had nothing except my briefcase. A fresh road kill or a wounded animal was not something I was too keen to put inside my briefcase.

I approached the animal that lay by the side of the road. It was a large male tayra who was alive but bleeding slightly through the nose and seemingly unconscious. I checked to see if the car tires had gone over him, but the animal seemed intact. His right leg was bent at a weird angle. I checked to see if it was broken and was relieved to learn that it wasn't.

Michelle approached slowly, her hands covering her mouth.

"Is it dead?" she asked, turning and making a guttural "eeew!" when she saw the small pool of blood.

"I think I nicked it with the bumper, but it doesn't seem too hurt," I said, trying to believe my own words. I absolutely hate to kill an animal on the road, and blame was already starting to come over me. Was I going too fast? Could I have avoided hitting it? However, I took the opportunity to take a close look at this common but not often seen animal. His coat was jet black, with a white patch of fur that ran from the base of his mouth over the chest and down to part of the belly. His head was flat and elongated, with big round ears and large canines that could surely give a nasty bite. He had large exposed claws on all four legs and a very long bushy tail covered with black stiff hairs. He looked like an oversized weasel. He also had a strong, musky smell.

Grabbing his tail and rear legs I tried to pull him off the road. The animal reacted by digging his front claws into the pavement and grunting loudly, making me jump back. I heard the car door shut behind me. No help was forthcoming from Michelle, I thought. The tayra was still alive, though not able to get up. I decided to mark the place where I hit it and leave it there to see if it recovered. On our way back from the meeting, we would stop. If it was dead, I would collect it and preserve it. If it was not there, then perhaps it had survived. Using one of my shoelaces to pull the tayra, I carefully dragged the animal off the road and into the road-side vegetation. Michelle was not very happy about the whole thing, and neither was I.

Six hours later, on our way back from town, we stopped at the site of the accident. We got out and started searching for the tayra, without success. Suddenly, right at the same place where it had jumped into the road before, the tayra crossed the road going the other way, limping on three legs, but seemingly recovered from its ordeal. It ran very fast up an exposed hill and disappeared behind some trees. We both felt much better. That was one specimen I was glad I didn't have to collect.   C. DE LA R.

The cream-colored throat patch on tayras can extend to the face and head.

TAXONOMY AND RELATIVES

The tayra was first described by Linnaeus in 1758 under the genus *Mustela*, but it was later awarded its own generic status. It has been at one time or another placed under several different genera, among them *Galera, Gulo, Mustela, Viverra,* and the invalid genus *Tayra.* It is related to the long-tailed weasel (*Mustela frenata*), the grison (*Galictis vittata*), the Neotropical river otter (*Lontra longicaudis*), and the skunks (*Spilogale, Conepatus,* and *Mephitis*). In appearance it is often confused with the jaguarundi (*Herpailurus yaguarondi*) or with black forms of other cat species.

COMMON NAMES

Tayra, eira; cadejo, lepasil (Honduras); tolomuco (Costa Rica); comadreja (Venezuela; cabeza de viejo (literally "old man's head," referring to the white hair around the head and neck of some populations) (Mexico, South America); eirá, cabeza blanca (literally "white head,") (Mexico). It is also called "tree otter" in some parts of its range.

DESCRIPTION

The tayra owes many of its common names to a characteristic white pelage covering the head, neck, and part of the back and shoulders, although this color pattern is highly variable and localized. Tayras are mostly black, brown, or grizzled gray, with a small white patch on their chests, the above-mentioned white crown, or no white hairs at all. Black or dark individuals are often confused with jaguarundis or melanistic (black) forms of margays or ocelots. There are also very light-colored individuals within normal-colored populations in some parts of South America. The pelage is rather coarse, short on head and neck, and long on the tail.

Tayras have a long body and head, ranging from 56 to 68 cm, and a tail that measures from 35 to 47 cm. They weigh around 4 to 5 kg, with males distinctively larger than females. Their characteristic flat, robust head and round, smallish ears gives them an appearance halfway between a cat and a small dog, although they are related to neither. They closely resemble the fisher of boreal forests of North America. The claws are nonretractile and very strong, and the soles of the feet are bare.

DENTAL FORMULA

I3/3, C1/1, P3/4, M1/1, for a total of 34 teeth.

HABITAT AND DISTRIBUTION

Tayras are fairly arboreal, requiring some kind of forest cover to survive. They

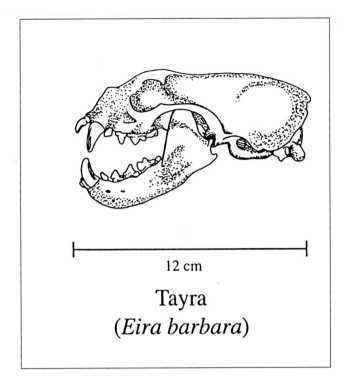

12 cm

Tayra
(*Eira barbara*)

14. *Historical (light) and present (dark) tayra distribution.*

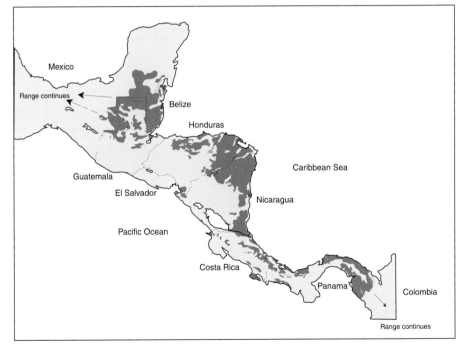

Tayra sniffing the air. Notice weasel-like features.

are found in primary and secondary forests, gallery forests (along streams and rivers), and deciduous forests, but they also make excursions into plantations, gardens, and other agricultural areas. They are found from central Mexico to northern Argentina (on the island of Trinidad) at elevations normally below 2,500 meters. Some sources report them at elevations of 1,200 meters and below (Eisenberg, 1989).

BEHAVIOR

Tayras are mainly crepuscular and diurnal, but this can vary depending on the densities of the prey species and on how close they live to humans. Tayras are surprisingly agile climbers and spend a fair amount of time in trees. One specimen observed in Costa Rica ran along the ground and climbed straight up the bole of a tree, disappearing between the lowbranches. It reappeared in the upper parts of the tree, moving confidently along the thin branches. Then it jumped to another close tree like a monkey, climbed down, and disappeared again among the forest floor vegetation. They

Profile of a young tayra.

*Tayra
walking
on a tree
branch.*

seem just as comfortable on the ground, where they can be observed hunting
small animals with amazing speed. They have been reported to hunt in
groups, but we have only observed them alone or at the most in pairs, foraging separately but within sight and hearing distance of each other. Their diet
consists of rodents, birds, invertebrates, eggs, fruit, nuts, and honey, and
they are probably responsible for some domestic fowl raids as well. We have
seen tayras in abandoned cacao plantations near urban areas in northern
Costa Rica.

Tayras can be tamed and make interesting but fairly destructive pets.
They communicate with a variety of grunts, growls, and hisses. They can
live up to 18 years in captivity, and reports indicate that they were at some
point domesticated and used by indigenous Americans as hunting companions (Grzimek, 1975).

REPRODUCTION

There are few published studies of tayras in scientific literature, and most
reproductive work has been done on captive animals. Tayras build nests or
dens in tree holes, hollow logs, or abandoned burrows where they have one

to three young after a gestation period of about 65 to 70 days. The young seem fairly precocious and are able to go out with the mother at about two months of age, although the few available observations do not entirely agree with each other. Reproductive habits in the wild are practically unknown.

CONSERVATION STATUS

Tayras are unprotected over most of Central America, with the exception of Honduras, which lists it under CITES Appendix II. In spite of their wide distribution and relative abundance, habitat destruction and deforestation is taking its toll on tayras. They should be considered threatened in many parts of their range. Even though their fur is of little value, they are hunted near populated areas because of their unproven role as an agricultural pest.

HOODED SKUNK

(Mephitis macroura)

We were following the narrow dirt path that led to the old house that was our temporary "laboratory in the bush." Dirk, my assistant, was a American zoology student volunteering in the Guanacaste National Park Project, where I was initiating preliminary research in aquatic insect communities. It was his first visit to the tropics, and over the last few days he had been continuously fascinated by the abundant fauna that lived along the rivers and streams we were studying. Our days were spent sampling streams for aquatic insects, collecting larvae from the bottom of the streams, and sweeping the stream-side vegetation with nets, catching adult insects that rested there. Every other night we would set up a white bed sheet between two trees or poles near a stream, place a pair of fluorescent lights in front of it, and spend most of the night catching adult aquatic insects that were attracted to the light. At dawn, after collecting the last insects, we would pick up our gear and head for the house, to preserve, label, and pin the night's catch. Then we would sleep until noon when the next cycle would begin in a different stream.

During our early morning walks, we would often encounter other creatures of the night that were also returning to their daytime resting places after a night of hunting or foraging. On this particular day, the smell of a skunk reached our noses well before we saw it walking along the trail in our direction. Having been raised on a farm in northern Pennsylvania, Dirk had encountered skunks before. His reaction was one of immediate alarm.

Portrait of an adult hooded skunk.

"Whoa!" he said. "We'd better get out of this guy's path on the double!"

"What's the problem?" I asked, curious at his reaction to the neat little black-and-white creature that continued its wobbly walk toward us, still unaware of our presence. I wanted to take a closer look, and perhaps even take some pictures. Dirk answered me by pulling me off the trail and moving swiftly toward the tangled brush that flanked the narrow path. I was more concerned about snakes in the tangle than by a little skunk that seemed to be minding its own business, but Dirk was adamantly concerned.

"If he gets near enough to spray you, I quit!" he informed me. "I'm not getting in the same house with you if you get peed on."

I shook him loose and went back to the trail. I intersected the path of the approaching skunk and waited for it to get closer. I had my camera ready to snap a couple of pictures, wondering if it would perform its well-known defensive routine of standing on its two front legs and pointing its rear end at the possible threat. (I later found that it is another species, the spotted skunk, *Spilogale putorius*, that carries on its defense in this most acrobatic fashion.)

The little skunk continued to walk toward me with its nose close to the ground, sniffing the dusty soil and looking this way and that every few steps. It became aware of me when it was about 10 feet away; it stopped, lifted its head, and became wary, sniffing the air in an attempt to decide if I was something to be concerned about or not. I had the "advantage" of having the wind blowing toward me (not a real advantage in front of a skunk), so for a while it couldn't figure out the nature of the road block that laid ahead.

As I moved into position for a close-up picture, it gave a little jump backwards, turned around, and lifted its tail straight up into the air. Behind me I heard Dirk's unprintable expletive. You would have thought the skunk had pulled a loaded gun on me. The skunk didn't raise onto its front legs, but it followed my now careful moves with its rear end, looking over its shoulder as if to keep me in its sight. My attention became focused on that little round pink spot of the skunk's anatomy. Could I duck or dodge a direct hit if things got nasty? Probably not.

Dirk was now in a quiet frenzy, waving at me to come over the bush as if my life was about to end. Snapping a last picture, I slowly moved backwards, concerned now that any sudden moves might trigger the impending catastrophe Dirk was so worried about. As I stepped gingerly off the trail, the skunk straightened out, rushed past our hiding place, and went out of sight.

Dirk's final comment to me was, "Next time you want to play Russian roulette with a loaded skunk, please keep me out of it." Hearing his stories of other people's too-close encounters with skunks took most of the remaining day. C. DE LA R.

TAXONOMY AND RELATIVES

There are three species of skunks that can be found in Central America. The hooded skunk, *Mephitis macroura*, is perhaps the most common one of all and is closely related to the American striped skunk (*Mephitis mephitis*). Several species of skunks range throughout the Neotropics and in North America. The spotted skunk (*Spilogale putorius*) is much smaller and its white markings are scattered around its body. The hog-nosed skunk (*Conepatus semistriatus*) is larger and has a characteristic long and hairless nose. Its back and the top of its tail are almost always completely white.

COMMON NAMES

Zorrillo ("little fox"), zorrillo listado, mofeta rayada, zorrillo encapuchado, zorro hediondo ("stinking fox"), zorro meón (literally "pissing fox," although it is not a fox and its musk does not come from its urine) (Spanish); skink, hooded skunk (English).

DESCRIPTION

The hooded skunk owes its name to the fact that its neck hair is arranged in a ruff. The head-body length of this skunk is 28 to 38 cm, and it weighs between 1.3 and 3 kg. Covered with bushy long fur, the body looks rather large and roundish, with short legs and a proportionally small head. The tail is very long, usually longer than its body, and is carried upright most of the time. It is very bushy, with longer hair at the base and shorter hair toward the tip. The ears are small and round and the snout is pointed.

The skunks, like all mustelids, have five toes on the front and hind paws. They have smooth, leathery palms and a plantigrade gait. Their front feet have long claws, which they use for digging. Generally, their feet are very small.

Two generally accepted color patterns are recognized in this species, although there are many variations. One variant shows an almost completely white back, including the tail. The other variant is almost completely black, including the tail, with two white stripes along the sides. Neither variant shows the characteristic white "V" found on the back of the striped skunk (*Mephitis mephitis*), its closest relative, which is well distributed in the United States and Canada but absent in Central and South America. Color patterns on both species vary greatly, although the striped skunk tends to have more white markings. I have seen several specimens of hooded skunks that are almost completely black; this seldom occurs in the striped skunk.

DENTAL FORMULA
I3/3, C1/1, P3/3, M1/2, for a total of 34 teeth.

HABITAT AND DISTRIBUTION
They are found in many different habitats and, as with other skunks, can often be seen close to human habitations and farms.

BEHAVIOR
Skunks do not "spray urine" as is commonly believed. The powerful-smelling substance is a solution of sulfur and alcohol, produced in special glands on the sides of the anus. The substance is chemically known as n-Butyl Mercaptan, although several related chemical compounds are actually present, their proportions and compositions varying between the different skunk species. It is sprayed with great accuracy through nozzlelike ducts. These nozzles are usually retracted into the anus and exposed when the need arises. The accuracy with which it is sprayed is remarkable, and its range is from four to up to seven meters, though it is more accurate at closer range. The smell can be detected by humans for up to half a mile away. Most skunks give a warning before spraying: they stamp their front feet and walk rather stiff-legged with a

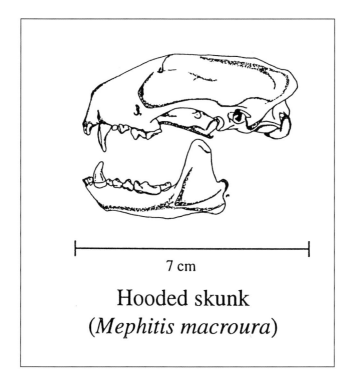

7 cm

Hooded skunk
(*Mephitis macroura*)

15. *Historical and present hooded skunk distribution.*

*Rear view of a
hooded skunk. This
is a warning pose.*

Baby hooded skunk.

raised tail. The animal itself is not smelly, although the scent can often be detected in unruffled animals. In aggressive encounters, however, they may spray one another.

Indigenous people in the Americas used to eat skunks, being careful to remove the scent glands first. The n-Butyl Mercaptan is poisonous, attacking the nervous system if ingested, and it can cause death. A direct hit could cause temporary blindness and vomiting, and the smell is extremely hard to remove. A wide variety of "recipes" have been proposed to clean the smell from animals and humans alike, including the classic "tomato juice bath," canning vinegar, and several commercially available (in the United States) formulas. Once the smell is in clothes or objects, it can be extremely difficult to eliminate; even when the smell is gone in dry objects, rewetting activates the smell again, even years after the spray.

Hooded skunks appear to be mainly nocturnal, but are also found moving during dawn and dusk, either coming or going to dens or day resting areas. The males maintain territories that overlap with those of the females, but not with territories of other males. They feed on small mammals, insects and other invertebrates, eggs, and fruit.

REPRODUCTION

Hooded skunks have one litter per year. North American individuals of this species usually mate between February and March, but it is not clear if the Central American populations follow this pattern. Four to eight blind young (called kits or kittens) are born after a gestation period of about 63 days. The ability to spray is developed at less than one month of age. After six to eight weeks the kittens start to follow their mother, usually walking in a single file. Males don't appear to take part in the upbringing of the young and have been observed behaving very aggressively toward females with young, possibly even killing them.

CONSERVATION STATUS

In the United States, skunks are seldom kept as pets because they are a frequent carrier of rabies. In some parts of their range they are trapped for their fur. They rarely attack poultry or other domestic animals, and they actually can be helpful in the control of rodents around houses and farms. They do not have any specific protection status in Central America.

SPOTTED SKUNK
(Spilogale putorius)

The little skunk stopped under the porch light by the door and sniffed the air. Finding the smell to its liking, it strolled confidently inside the house toward the table where I had been transcribing my field notes into my journal. I slowly raised my feet and placed them quietly on the table, wondering if the skunk had noticed my presence or if it would become alarmed. It walked right under my chair and made its way toward the cluttered kitchen.

I was staying at a biologist's house in the Santa Rosa National Park, in northern Costa Rica, during a spell of dry weather in June. The owners of the house were away for a few weeks, and they were allowing me to use their house, library, and computer to wrap up a three-month stint where I had begun my research in aquatic ecosystems. The house was old and crammed with field gear, specimens, and books. It was literally open to any creature that wanted to come in and investigate this most peculiar habitat. Tucked away in a little patch of thick vegetation, it was home to a large resident fauna. Bats hung from some of the exposed rafters. Sometimes they hung over the small cot I was using to sleep on and provided gratuitous excitement at all hours of the night. In the kitchen, a resident boa constrictor rested between the zinc roof and the wood rafters. Three bulges were evidence of recent rodent meals. Frogs lived and mated in the shower stall. A marsupial mouse nightly scuttled around the cupboards. Sometimes a small baby clung to her, attached to her tit as she ran around the kitchen. Scorpions and spiders completed the menagerie. This made every common activity, such as putting on shoes or picking up a towel, a chancy and often exciting event.

The little skunk walked straight to the kitchen, found the garbage pail, and jumped inside it, its tail sticking up like a little flag over the lip of the can. Obviously it had been here before, because it knew exactly where to go. I put my feet down and observed its foraging. It dug through the garbage, picking up egg shells and the remains of last night's chicken dinner. Crunching noises filled the room for a few minutes. Satisfied, it climbed out of the pail and quickly explored the rest of the house. Finally, it approached the table and sat right over my boot (which I happened to be wearing at the time). It licked its paws and looked around while I held my breath. I was surprised by its tameness and its lack of odor (which wasn't the reason why I was holding my breath). Its black fur was peppered with white splotches and looked soft and silky, although I wasn't about to attempt to confirm my visual impressions. After its manicure was over, it ambled out of the door and into the darkness.   C. DE LA R.

TAXONOMY AND RELATIVES

There are two species of *Spilogale*, only one of which, *Spilogale putorius*, is found in Central America. It is closely related to the hooded skunk (*Mephitis macroura*) and the hog-nosed skunks (*Conepatus* spp.).

Portrait of an adult spotted skunk.

COMMON NAMES

Spotted skunk, civet, hydrophobia cat (United States); zorro, zorro meón (Costa Rica); zorrillo mofeta.

DESCRIPTION

The spotted skunk is the smallest of the Central American skunks. Its head to body length ranges from 12 to 34 cm. The tail is between 9 and 23 cm long and is usually shorter than the head-body length, but it has very long hair. Weighing 0.5 to 1 kg, the male is distinctly larger than the female, which usually weighs under 0.5 kg. The body of the spotted skunk is more delicate looking than that of other species, having a squirrellike appearance.

Its background color is black with a white tail tip. There is generally a small white spot on the forehead and under each ear. There are also four broken stripes along the back, neck, and sides. The body has a more splotchy than striped appearance. The proportions of black and white vary considerably, but the pattern is very distinct and not found in any of the other skunks. The fur is also much finer than in the other skunks. Individuals can be easily distinguished from each other by the variation of their white and black markings.

In comparison, the hooded skunk, *Mephitis macroura*, has a longer tail and is much bigger and striped, not spotted. The even larger hog-nosed skunk (*Conepatus semistriatus*) possesses the typical naked nose, no spots, and an entirely or nearly white tail and back.

DENTAL FORMULA

I3/3, C1/1, P3/3, M1/2, for a total of 34 teeth.

HABITAT AND DISTRIBUTION

The spotted skunk is found from southwest Canada to Costa Rica. It occupies many different habitats and, as with other skunks, can often be seen close to human habitations and farms.

BEHAVIOR

Spotted skunks adopt a unique handstand position as part of their defense. It is a warning not to come any closer and shows clearly a frontal view of the whole body of the individual. If the handstand fails to have any effect on the aggressor, the spotted skunk will arch his back over its head and direct a shot of noxious spray at the victim. The spray of skunks is very well aimed, often at the face of its pursuer. Strong smelling and toxic, if it gets into the eyes it can cause temporary blindness. Also refer to the hooded skunk for more information about spray.

These skunks are mainly active at dusk and dawn, but can be seen active at all times. Normally they are terrestrial but sometimes climb trees, especially if in danger. Spotted skunks nest in burrows, hollow trees, logs, under roots or piles of rocks, and sometimes under old houses.

The spotted skunk is a skillful little hunter and its diet consists of small mammals, invertebrates, birds, eggs, lizards, and fruits. It also eats snakes and there is evidence that it might be resistant to the venom of rattlesnakes.

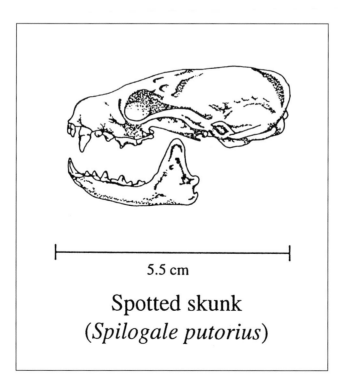

5.5 cm

Spotted skunk
(*Spilogale putorius*)

Handstand position of a spotted skunk.

REPRODUCTION

It is not clear if the Central American spotted skunk has a set breeding season. In the northern part of its range, the young are reported to be born between May and June. The female has eight or 10 mammae, and on average two to six young are born after a gestation period of 120 days or more. They are weaned at about two months of age.

Baby spotted skunk sleeping.

CONSERVATION STATUS

Spotted skunks are trapped in some parts of their range for their fur but have become rare and protected in northern parts of their North American range; changing land use provides less habitat for a preferred food—house mice which infest old-fashioned corn cribs and granaries. They can be very beneficial if left to live undisturbed, especially around buildings, as they kill mice and rats and can help control these pests around farms and silos. They are not offered any special type of protection in Central America.

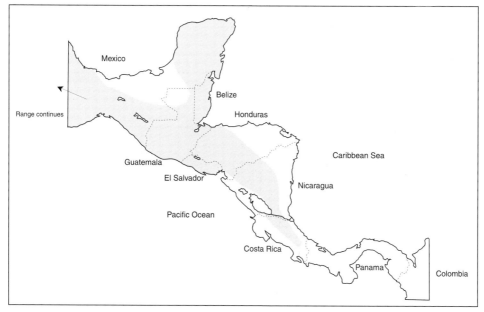

16. *Historical and present spotted skunk distribution.*

HOG-NOSED SKUNKS

(Conepatus semistriatus and *C. mesoleucus)*

Portrait of a hog-nosed skunk. Notice the large nose and claws.

The new nature trail of the Heliconia Biological Field Station was a one kilo-meter–long winding path through primary and secondary forest on the north-ern slope of the Tenorio Volcano, in northern Costa Rica. This area is covered by very humid rain forest, and sunny days are almost cause for celebration. The moss-covered trees continuously dripped from what is called "cloud drip": water condensing on leaves and branches as the low clouds sweep through the forest. The forest floor is spongy and squishy and is a great sub-strate for countless grubs and other invertebrates. On the edges of the forests, the wind moves the clouds faster and a person can get very wet just standing in the path.

Claudia and I were standing at the end of the trail as we reviewed our day's observations of flora and fauna for an interpretative trail guide. All along the trail we found places where animals had scratched and dug for edible prey un-derneath. At night, nine-banded armadillos (*Dasypus novemcinctus*) rooted along the trail, especially along the edges of the forest. These edges, techni-cally referred to as "ecotones," usually show a higher number of species than individual ecosystems. Actually, some species prefer to live on these edges.

We finished our work and walked back on the trail. We wanted to make some nighttime observations of the armadillos foraging. Hearing soft grunts and digging noises, we shut off the flashlight and walked carefully toward the noise. Since armadillos hear well but are not known for their keen eyesight, we walked slowly along the trail, stopping when the digging noises stopped and resuming when we thought the animal was busy digging again. Finally, I turned on my flashlight and, covering most of the beam with my hand, pointed a feeble ray of light toward the alleged armadillo.

I heard Claudia gasp at the same time as I did. Our armadillo was actually a large skunk! It was larger and more robust than other skunks I had seen be-fore. It was planted on its four feet, head held high, sniffing the air. It was probably deciding what to do to these two intruders. There was what looked like a large beetle larva protruding from its mouth. The smell and taste of the juicy larva probably helped distract it from our approach. We were no more than a few feet from it, and we were able to take a good look at his features (including getting a positive gender ID once it turned around and walked away).

The most striking feature was his very large and callous-looking nose on a long, pointed black face. There was a lot of white on his body, starting on the top of the head and running to the tail. There was a broad black band framed by white along his back. The front claws were enormous—good tools for an animal that makes a living digging insects from the soil and forest litter. All

Profile of a hog-nosed skunk.

these characteristics identified him as a hog-nosed skunk. Claudia and I started to back up slowly, concerned about the legendary defense mechanism which we didn't want to experience. I had already had enough close encounters with skunks to know better than to disturb them. The skunk stomped the ground with his paws a couple of times, keeping his tail up but safely pointed away from us.

The skunk turned around and walked back along the trail. We looked at each other and decided to follow it. As long as the tail was kept low we felt relatively safe. The skunk had a different idea. As soon as we caught up with him, he stopped and turned his back toward us. He raised his tail, stomped the ground, and growled softly with his mouth half closed. This was enough for us. We took the hint and retreated again.   C. DE LA R.

TAXONOMY AND RELATIVES

There are five species of *Conepatus* in the Americas. Two of them are present in Central America, *Conepatus mesoleucus* and *Conepatus semistriatus*. They are closely related to the other two genera, the spotted skunk (*Spilogale*) and the striped skunk (*Mephitis*). However, there has been a fairly active reorganization of skunk taxonomy in the last few years, and several species of these genera have been split or lumped together, depending on which source is consulted. Most of the taxonomic problems are confined to whether two or more species should be considered subspecies or variants of a single species, or if the differences found in coloration, behavior, or other characteristics are unique enough to warrant different species status.

Our feeling is that color patterns, commonly used in the determination of species, are highly variable throughout the range of most species, with many versions within and between populations. We use here the species recognized by Wozencraft (1995).

COMMON NAMES

Hog-nosed skunk, common hog-nosed skunk (*C. mesoleucus*), striped hog-nosed skunk (*C. semistriatus*), rooter skunk; zorrillo de espalda blanca, zorrillo, zorro coleto, zorrillo cadeno, zorro hediondo (Spanish); gato cañero, gato de caña (Panama); zorrillo de capucha (Honduras).

DESCRIPTION

Hog-nosed skunks obtained their name from their conspicuous pig-like nose, which is fairly long and, for about 25 mm, hairless and black. The fur is coarser than in the other skunk species, fairly long on the body and particularly long on the tail. The crown, back, and tail are white, while the face, legs, and underside are black.

Apparently, the two species of hog-nosed skunks found in Central America do not overlap in their range. *Conepatus mesoleucus*, the common hog-nosed skunk, has a white tail and a broad white stripe that covers most of its back. *Conepatus semistriatus*, the striped hog-nosed skunk, has two white stripes on its back.

Of the other two species of skunks in Central America, the one most similar to the hog-nosed skunks is the hooded skunk, *Mephitis macroura*, which has a longer tail. If there is white on the back, it is generally mixed with black. The other skunk species in Central America, the spotted skunk (*Spilogale putorius*), is smaller and has a very distinct spotty pattern. Neither of the other species has the naked nose or a white tail.

The head and body length of this skunk is from 35 to 48 cm, with a tail of 18 to 30 cm. Hog-nosed skunks are the largest of the Central American species, weighing between 2 and 4.5 kg.

DENTAL FORMULA

I/3, C1/1, P2 or 3/3, M1/2, for a total of 32 to 34 teeth. (Note: there seems to

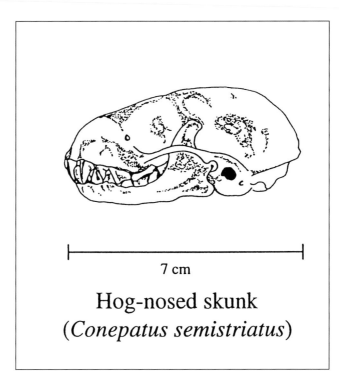

Hog-nosed skunk
(Conepatus semistriatus)

7 cm

be some disagreement among authors on the total number of teeth for this species.)

HABITAT AND DISTRIBUTION

Conepatus mesoleucus can be found from the southern United States to Nicaragua. *Conepatus semistriatus* is distributed further south, from Mexico to Peru and parts of Brazil. They are found in a variety of habitats, from primary to secondary forests and disturbed areas, up to 4,000 meters. They seem to prefer more open areas and can even be found close to human habitations.

BEHAVIOR

The hog-nosed skunk is thought to be mainly nocturnal but can also be seen at dusk, dawn, and rarely in the day. It feeds mainly on invertebrates, but also consumes mollusks, eggs, small mammals, reptiles, fruits, nuts, and sometimes snakes. In the Andes it has been reported to be resistant to the venom of pit vipers. It spends quite a bit of its time rooting in the soil and leaf litter for insects. For this it uses its nose and front paws which have very long claws. They are almost three times as long as those on the hind feet. *Conepatus* tends to move more slowly than the other two species and is very terrestrial, seldom climbing trees. It often moves alone and its dens are usually found in crevices in rock cliffs, hollow logs, or dens made by other animals. Also refer to the hooded skunk for more information.

REPRODUCTION

In the northern parts of their range, hog-nosed skunks mate in February and two to four young are born in April or May. In the southern parts of their range there might be no clear breeding season. Females have only six mammae.

CONSERVATION STATUS

The fur of this skunk is of little value because it is coarser than in the other skunk species. However, they are still hunted in some countries. Apparently there is no protection status for this or other species of skunks in Central America.

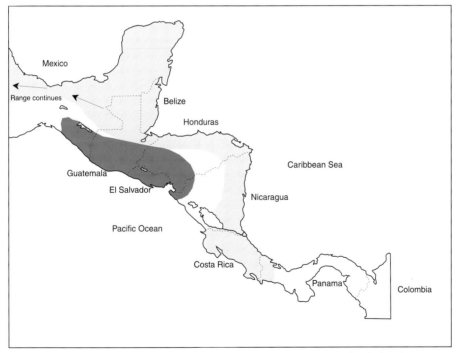

17. *Historical and present striped (light) and common (dark) hog-nosed skunk distribution.*

*Baby hog-nosed
skunk on a tree.*

GRISON

(Galictis vittata)

The grison made its appearance on the narrow trail Marvin Jiménez had cut
through the thick undergrowth a few days before in the forest covering the
Tenorio volcano in northern Costa Rica. From a distance, the grison looked
like an odd whitish-gray furry snake slithering down the muddy terrain and
sniffing the ground. Marvin stopped and waited for it to approach, his long
machete on the ready in case the animal decided to attack him. As it got
closer, more of its features became clear. The short, squatty-looking legs gave
it a characteristic shuffling gait. It had dark, stiff fur below and to the sides of
the lighter back. It produced grunting sounds while foraging. About 50 feet
from where Marvin was standing, the grison stopped and commenced digging
furiously under the forest litter. Its huge claws tore the ground and dug deep,
and while digging it made short snuffling and grunting sounds. It was so in-
tent on its digging that Marvin was able to get within 10 feet of it before it
became aware of him. The grison stopped digging and lifted its flat broad
head. Its large ears moved as it sniffed the air. Sight must not have been its

strongest sense, because it took it a couple of minutes to become alarmed, emit a loud growl, and retreat rapidly along the trail where it came from.

Marvin, a local farmer, knew Tenorio and its secrets well. He had lived for many years in the area while farming and raising a family. When he settled with his wife in the region 16 years ago, Tenorio had been completely covered with primary humid forests. There were only dirt and gravel roads in the area. A trip from the Inter American Highway and the nearest town of Cañas, in the Pacific northwest, could take from several hours to a couple of days. However, there was a small settler's colony getting started near the small town of Bijagua. The town was named for a plant in the Heliconia family that produces beautiful yellow flowers and is commonly found along streams and rivers. The settlement was part of a government-supported rural revitalization plan, and land was offered to would-be farmers at almost no cost. They had to settle it, cut the forest down, plant a few crops, and make a living from the sale of produce, fruits, cattle, or whatever the farmer chose to produce.

In spite of being a farmer under such circumstances, Marvin had a tremendous love for wild places, and this place was wild. He would take long hikes through the nearly untouched forest. He explored the old water-filled crater, with its thermal springs, ravines, and razorback ridges. Sometimes he hunted the abundant wildlife to bring food to the table. Most of the time he simply observed and admired the wildlife.

The forests of Tenorio are now protected under the National Parks Service, and Marvin manages a small biological field station and ecotourism project on the buffer zone of the newly created park. He is a leading member of the local conservation community and dedicated to the protection of grisons and all other animals and plants of the region. Grisons now thrive in the forests of Tenorio, and Marvin thrives on his wildlife encounters. He appreciates the benefits that wildlife have brought to his family and to the settlement through ecotourism and scientific research.   C. DE LA R.

TAXONOMY AND RELATIVES

There are two species in the genus *Galictis*, the greater grison, *G. vittata*, and the little grison, *G. cuja*. Only the greater grison is found in Central America; its closest relative, the little grison, is only found in parts of South America. Grisons are related to the tayra (*Eira barbara*), the weasels, and the skunks, although they are very distinct from all of them. It is an easy animal to identify in the field, for there is no other similar species in the region.

COMMON NAMES

Grison, grisón (Spanish); hurón; tejón; lobo gallinero, tigrillo rosillo (Panama);

*Adult grison
sitting on a log.*

zorro camacita (Venezuela); rey de las ardillas (literally, "king of the squirrels")
(Mexico).

DESCRIPTION

The grison has a head-body length of 47 to 55 cm, with a short tail measuring
about one third of the head-body length. It weighs between 1.4 and 3.3 kg.
Grisons have a similar body pattern to weasels (*Mustela*), with an elongated
and fairly thin body and very short legs. The head is also flattened, and the
neck is long and as thick as the head, with small dark eyes. The lower part of
the face, throat, chest, legs, and feet are black. The upper part of the body and
the crown of the head are grizzled gray. Just above the eyes there is a small
white head stripe going down half of the neck, so that the small white ears are
not very visible, blending in with the white head stripe. The fur is fairly long,
especially on the grizzled body and tail. Interestingly, the feet of the grison are
partly webbed, although this feature is not often reported. They growl and
grunt when disturbed or attacked and can be very fast in retreat or in attack.

DENTAL FORMULA

I3/3, C1/1, P3/4, M1/1, for a total of 34 teeth.

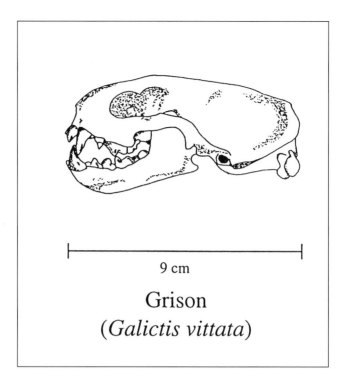

9 cm

Grison
(*Galictis vittata*)

HABITAT AND DISTRIBUTION

Galictis vittata, the greater grison, can be found from southern Mexico to Brazil and Peru. It is found in nearly all types of habitats, from tropical forests to grasslands and even cultivated areas, although not in great numbers.

BEHAVIOR

Grisons can be active in the day or night. They are very opportunistic with their diet, eating whatever is available. They probably fit their activity patterns around those of their most dominant prey species at the time. They are mainly terrestrial, but can climb quite well. With their semiwebbed feet, they seem to be quite good swimmers and divers and can often be seen near rivers and streams. Their diet ranges from small mammals, birds, amphibians, reptiles, eggs, and invertebrates to nuts and fruits. They can move fast and are very agile. They travel in pairs or alone, though they can also be seen in small groups, probably consisting of females with young.

*Adult
grison
growling.*

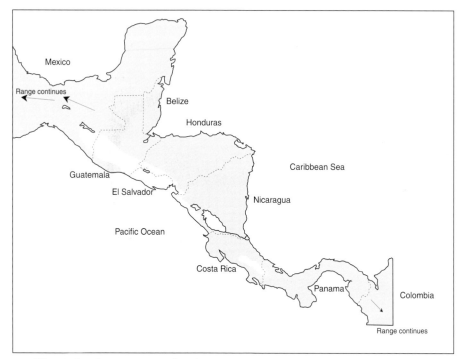

18. *Historical and present grison distribution.*

They den in hollow logs or trees, under tree roots, in small caves between the rocks, or in burrows either made by them or other animals, sometimes their own victims. They follow their prey into burrows and either kill them there or flush them out to kill them.

REPRODUCTION

Not much is known about their reproduction apart from the fact that they seem to have a litter size of two to four young.

CONSERVATION STATUS

Grisons are listed under CITES Appendix III for Costa Rica, although they seem to be widespread and fairly common in some areas of this country. Their real status in the region is not known.

In some parts of their range the males are trapped for their body parts that are believed by some locals to have aphrodisiac qualities. They are also sold as pets or used like ferrets for hunting.

Young grison coming out from under a tree.

LONG-TAILED WEASEL

(Mustela frenata)

Young weasel inspecting a ladybug.

The racket in the chicken coop was unbelievable. It started with a series of sleepy-sounding clucks that soon turned into an agitated commotion and finally total chaos. One scream rose over the hullabaloo and then got choked off. During the few minutes that it took me to wake up, get some clothes on, and search for my flashlight (there was no electricity at the house at that time), I crashed into my host, who was also doing what I was doing, and ran out the door and through the yard to the coop as the frenzy died off. The fearsome predator had found its way into the cage and one by one had disposed of all the chicks and the hens. When we got to the coop only the rooster was standing, quite shaken by the ordeal and a little ruffled, but physically unharmed.

The inspection revealed the unmistakable signature of the hunter: dead bodies strewn all around, their heads chewed up or severed off. It was the gruesome scene of a serial killer's rampage.

I was staying at the farm of friends in northern Costa Rica. They raised chickens for eggs and meat. The dozen or so chickens and chicks roamed free during the day, eating dry corn, insects, seeds, and other tidbits. Later in the day they were fed leftovers, mostly rice and other table scraps. At the approach of dusk, the whole happy flock would file to the pen, a rough wooden cage closed off by thin chicken wire held together by pieces of string and staples. The arrangement worked fine to keep out opossums, feral dogs, and the occasional margay or tiger cat. This time, however, the chicken wire was not enough. The tiny hole in the corner of the cage was no larger than a silver dollar. That was the only hole needed, however, for a small predator. Outside the hole there were tiny tracks in the dust. How could such a little creature cause so much carnage? There was no other trace of the animal, but my friend identified it as a weasel.

Long-tailed weasels, as well as some of their northern relatives, are skilled and fierce predators. The case I had witnessed provided ample evidence of their killing competence, though sleeping chickens were easy targets for this seldom-seen hunter.   C. DE LA R.

"It was a few years ago and we were still at the old station in Las Flores when our cat Scaramouche had her young in our house," explained Sabine, the co-director of PROFELIS, the national cat rescue station in Costa Rica. We sat around the kitchen table one evening having fresh-brewed coffee at the new field station as she told us her story.

"Remember that patched-up hole near the stairs of the kitchen door in our house? We had taken a few boards off at the bottom to allow the cat to come in whenever she wanted," Sabine said.

Sure I remembered. I had worked as a research assistant at the old station; it was between the Tenorio and Miravalles volcanoes in northern Costa Rica and was quite wet most of the time, often raining for 10 or 12 days straight. Everything would become wet and smelly; clothes wouldn't dry and eventually began to grow a thin layer of mold. It was also hard on other residents of the station, including Nasi, the half-tame coati who lived around the house for a while, Freitag, the spider monkey, and all the cats. Scaramouche kept her kittens in the house, entering though the hole next to the kitchen door. She was a large black-and-white domestic cat who was always around to keep the kitchen area free of mice and other vermin.

"It was late morning," Sabine continued, "and I had just finished cleaning the cages and entered the house through the front door. I crossed the living room and went into the kitchen. I saw something moving on my left. When I turned I saw a tiny brown animal looking out from behind the refrigerator. The face was gray-brown and its front paws and neck were a light chestnut color, and it had a white throat and belly. It stared at me with dark little eyes. The small rounded ears pointed forward and the little whiskers were moving as its tiny pinkish-brown nose sniffed in the air." Sabine recognized it as the tiny but fierce long-tailed weasel.

"The cat, close at hand and in hope of catching some food, had not seen it yet," Sabine continued. "It was only a matter of time, since the only exit out of the kitchen was the hole near the kitchen door. To get there the weasel would have to run across the room past Scaramouche.

"For a few more seconds it stayed in this position as if trying to decide whether it was safe to continue hunting in the kitchen, or whether it was time to bolt and seek safer grounds. It turned around, jumped straight to the floor, and ran quickly toward the kitchen door in the characteristic miniature gallop of weasels.

"The cat turned her head and for about a second or two couldn't believe her luck. She bolted after the weasel, probably thinking it was some stretched-out rat or mouse. The little weasel was still not close enough to the hole to make a clean escape. It stopped, turned around, and met the attacking cat. It stood on its rear paws and emitted a loud high-pitched screech. The cat was totally thrown off by the unexpected response. The weasel took rapid advantage of the brief confusion and scampered through the hole. A very confused cat was left sitting on the kitchen floor, licking her paw and pretending nothing had happened," Sabine said. We laughed at this image of Scaramouche.

"She had lost the weasel," Sabine concluded, "but still kept her dignity!"

C. C. N.

TAXONOMY AND RELATIVES

The long-tailed weasel is the only species of the genus *Mustela* in Central America. It belongs to the subfamily Mustelinae, and its closest relatives are the tayra (*Eira barbara*) and the grison (*Galictis vittata*). It is also related to three species of skunks which belong to the subfamily Mephitinae. The genus *Mustela* was described by Linnaeus in 1758, and the species *Mustela frenata* was described by Lichtenstein in 1831 from Mexican specimens. The group is still going through revisions, mostly at the subgeneric levels.

COMMON NAMES

Long-tailed weasel; comadreja, saben, sebencito, hurón, onza, lince.

DESCRIPTION

The long-tailed weasel has a very elongated, thin body with a long neck that looks as thick as the head. In fact, the head, neck, and body of a stretched out weasel has a cylindrical or tubelike appearance. The head is flattened and round, with a blunt muzzle, large eyes, and round, fairly big forward-pointing ears. The legs are very short and the tail is thin, short-haired, and slightly wider at its base. It is about 50 to 60% of the head-body length.

*Adult weasel
sniffing the air.*

In Central America the head and body length of the long-tailed weasel is about 20 to 35 cm, and it has a weight of between 85 and 365 g. The males are distinctly larger than the females. Members of this species in northern latitudes tend to be smaller and also change their fur in the winter to a pure white (except the tip of the tail). The canine teeth are prominent and very sharp, and the carnassials have characteristic cutting edges.

DENTAL FORMULA

I3/3, C1/1, P3/3, M1/2, for a total of 34 teeth.

HABITAT AND DISTRIBUTION

The long-tailed weasel can be found from southern Canada to northern South America, from lowland forest to areas up to 4,000 meters. Preferring relatively open spaces, this weasel is often found in grasslands or bushy areas, but it occupies a wide variety of habitats. In drier areas, it likes to stay near water. It doesn't seem to mind living in proximity to human habitations, especially where rodent populations are large.

BEHAVIOR

Though weasels are more nocturnal, they can be active day and night. They are terrestrial hunters whose diet consists of small mammals up to the size of rabbits, invertebrates, birds, reptiles, nuts, eggs, and fruit. At times the prey animal might be much larger than the weasel. With its long, thin body it can pursue its prey to the end of a small burrow. The prey is usually killed by bites to the back of the neck and portions of its fur may be used to line the weasel's den. This den may even be the former burrow of its prey. They also den in tree holes, hollow logs, or among rocks.

A chicken house in the vicinity of a weasel's territory may result in the death of some or all of the chickens. The weasel can enter the chicken house through the tiniest hole. Once inside, its very strong drive to kill takes over, and, as a result, it may kill far more than it could ever eat. This habit has contributed to popular tales of weasels sucking the blood of their victims and leaving their carcasses intact. In reality, the weasel is simply overwhelmed by so many available chickens which can't escape like wild birds could. Occasionally farmers have found inside the coop a weasel asleep from the exhaustion of the night's work. In nature it would never come across such a vast amount of defenseless prey. The strong drive to kill could be a result of a great need for food due to its very high metabolic rate. *M. frenata* has a metabolic rate that is 50 to 100% higher than that of a less elongated animal of the same weight.

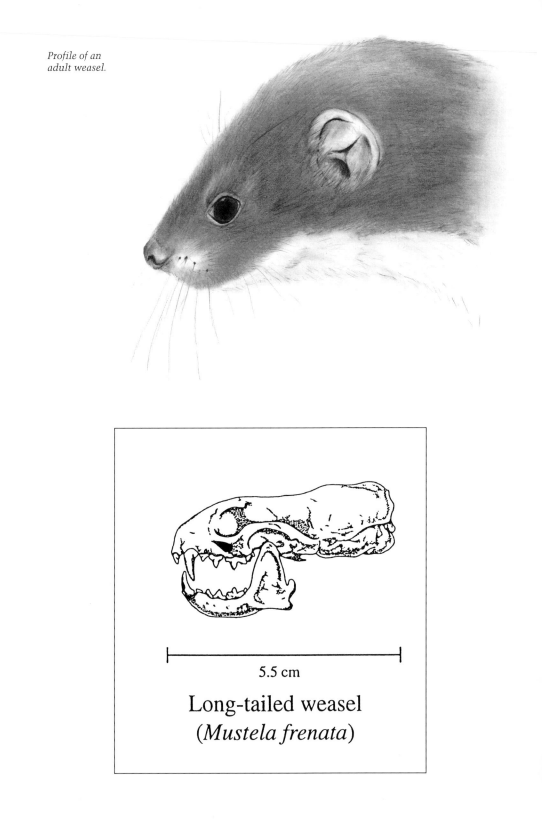

Profile of an adult weasel.

5.5 cm

Long-tailed weasel
(*Mustela frenata*)

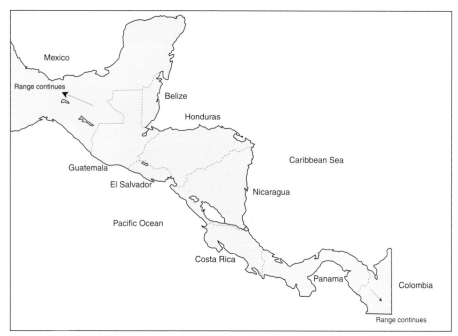

19. *Historical and present long-tailed weasel distribution.*

Long-tailed weasels are normally solitary. While the home ranges of opposite sexes overlap, those of the same sex do not. When alert they may sit up on their haunches for a short time and crane their necks in order to get a better view. If cornered, they sometimes attack even humans.

REPRODUCTION

In the northern parts of its range, mating occurs between July and August, but due to a delayed implantation, the fertilized egg does not start growing until March. This phenomenon has not been fully documented in tropical populations. About 27 days later three to nine young are born (although nine young might cause a bit of a problem, as the mother has only eight mammae). At birth the young weigh just over three grams. The female may even mate the same year she is born, sometimes when still a nestling herself, while the young males don't mature until the next year.

CONSERVATION STATUS

The long-tailed weasel, though a problem with chicken houses that are not well closed, can be very beneficial to humans. They are very good at controlling rats and mice. They are relatively common and abundant throughout their range and are not listed on any endangered or threatened list.

Baby weasel.

*Weasel
standing
on hind
legs.*

Neotropical river otter

(Lontra longicaudis)

Portrait of a river otter vocalizing.

The San Juan River forms the border between Costa Rica and Nicaragua for much of its 200 kilometers. It is a wide river full of history and conflict. In its waters and on its tributaries have fought the British, the Germans, the Americans, the Dutch, the Nicaraguans, and the Costa Ricans. They fought to gain control over transportation rights to this natural highway, to defend their rights against hostile takers in the name of national sovereignty, and to reap opportunities for quick wealth. It was the path of rubber, gold, and all types of merchandise and settlers.

Through its tributaries settlers reached deep into the unexplored jungle, clearing small patches of forest and forming the first towns. Greytown, Sarapiquí, Upala, Guatuso, Boca del San Carlos, and Los Chiles grew into port cities. The river connected them with the vast network of the first highways known to humans.

We drifted along a wide stretch of the Zapote River in Costa Rica on our way to Lake Nicaragua. I kept my eyes open for river otters, which I knew once thrived in these waters. I had seen them a few times in less disturbed rivers such as the Corobicí River, in Costa Rica's Guanacaste Province. One time a pair of adult otters spent almost an hour swimming, diving, and feeding on freshwater crabs in front of a group of diners at the Corobicí Restaurant near the Inter American Highway. I was encouraged to see them there because they are very rare and should be placed on the endangered species list for most of Central America. They have been hunted to near extirpation in some areas. However, the main reason for their disappearance has been river pollution, channelization, destruction of the gallery forests, and, to a lesser degree, the rural pet and skin trade.

I asked Raúl, our boater, if he had ever seen otters in this river. "Sure," he said, "there are lots around." However, "lots" has different meanings. Perhaps there were lots when he was growing up (he was in his late twenties). Perhaps when the region was mostly covered with forests there were lots. But certainly there were not so many now. I had traveled this river a dozen times and had yet to see one river otter swimming free.

Raúl pointed to a house about half a mile down the river. "There are otters there," he said. "They have one as a pet."

I asked him to stop at the house, so I could look at it and take some pictures.

The otter was there, all right. A small juvenile was tied to the rickety dock by a long string, which allowed it some degree of freedom around the dwelling. When we approached, the youngster was lying on its back on the shore, chewing and sucking at the rubber nipple of a plastic baby bottle half full of milk dexterously held in its front paws. Its slick body seemed almost polished and extremely aerodynamic. It had a thick, round, tapering tail which is one of the differences between this species and the South American giant river otter (*Pteronura brasiliensis*). That species is larger and has a rather flattened tail. Its other close relative, the Northern river otter, *Lontra canadensis*, has been intensely studied in comparison to its southern cousin. However, they share many traits and the same threats.

The playful young otter was sliding along the muddy bank and into the water where it would swim with an undulating movement by giving powerful thrusts with its tail. Webbed feet allowed it to maintain direction and aided in propulsion.

I asked the owners what had happened to its parents, for the parent-young bond is strong in this species. They said that the baby was found abandoned by the side of the river (an unlikely event) and that they had adopted it to raise it as a pet. I checked back about six months later and was told that the little otter had escaped.   C. DE LA R.

TAXONOMY AND RELATIVES

There seems to be a recent move to reclassify New World (the Americas) otters in the genus *Lontra*, which at some point was considered to be either a subgenus or simply part of the genus *Lutra*. Most of the current research sources list the four species of American otters within the genus *Lutra*. Wozencraft (1995), the most current taxonomic reference for the order Carnivora, places all American species in the genus *Lontra*. The five otter species are: the North American river otter (*Lontra canadensis*), the Neotropical river otter (*L. longicaudis*), the Giant river otter (*Pteronura brasiliensis*), the Southern

River otter lying down.

river otter (*L. provocax*), and the Marine otter (*L. felina*), of which only the Neotropical river otter is found in Central America. The true relationships of otters are still debatable, and future research is expected to bring more changes to this current arrangement.

Otters are placed within their own subfamily, Lutrinae, within the family Mustelidae. They are all closely associated with aquatic habitats and present a series of morphological and physiological characteristics unique among the mustelids.

COMMON NAMES

Neotropical river otter (United States); perro de agua, nutria (Venezuela, Costa Rica, Nicaragua); lobito de río común.

DESCRIPTION

Otters are the only amphibious species in the weasel family. They are dark grayish-brown on their backs and light brown underneath. Often they have one or more creamy-white splotches on the throat, although there appears to be a lot of variation throughout their range. When otters are dry, their fur feels very soft and velvety. When wet, however, it is water repellent due to the extremely dense underfur and long guard hairs. On the whole, their body has a very streamlined appearance which becomes more obvious when seen underwater. The head is flattened but rounded, and the transition between the head and the body is not very distinct, as the neck is short and thick. The body is elongated, with short legs and a very muscular tail, thick at its base and tapering toward the end. They are very well adapted to a life in the water and can close off their small ears and nostrils when diving. The muzzle is rather blunt with a wide nose, and there are many long, drooping sensitive whiskers. Like most other otters, Neotropical river otters possess strong claws and webbed feet. They also have paired scent glands at the base of the tail which produce a heavy musky smell.

Their head-body length ranges from 50 to 79 cm, with a tail from 38 to 57 cm long. They can weigh anywhere from 5 to 14 kg, with the males being larger than the females.

DENTAL FORMULA

I3/3, C1/1, P4/3, M1/2, for a total of 36 teeth.

HABITAT AND DISTRIBUTION

Lontra longicaudis is found in Central and South America, between Mexico and Argentina. It is found along clean rivers and streams near forests and rela-

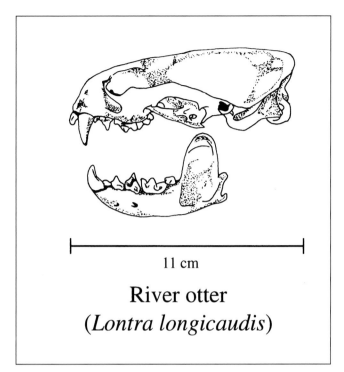

11 cm

River otter
(*Lontra longicaudis*)

20. *Historical and present Neotropical river otter distribution.*

tively undisturbed areas, although it has been exterminated throughout much of its former range.

BEHAVIOR

River otters are well known for their dexterity, using their "hands," or front paws, to manipulate objects, particularly food items. Sea otters (*Enhydra lutris*) are famous for their use of tools (stones over which they open abalones), an ability primarily reserved for primates and certain birds. River otters, while not known to use tools, do use their paws to search for food, which consists mainly of fish and crustaceans such as crayfish and freshwater crabs. Their habits are diurnal and nocturnal. They can be seen foraging or swimming alone or in pairs. They travel either as mated pairs or as mothers with young.

Vocalizations are multiple and varied in all species of otters, and Neotropical river otters are no exception. They can produce high-pitched loud whistles, screeches, and grunts, among other sounds. Agile and adept swimmers, they prefer to live in waters relatively clean and clear.

Portrait of two young otters.

*Adult river otter
with a recent catch.*

While much research has been done on the North American river otter (*L. canadensis*), very little is known of the Neotropical species. Given their close taxonomic relationship, many behavioral and physiological features of both species are assumed to be similar, but these assumptions need to be supported by research.

REPRODUCTION

This species is believed to have from one to four young (two or three on average) after an unknown gestation period. They have four mammae. Some reproductive features of the northern species (such as delayed implantation of the fertilized egg, which extends the gestation period) are not known to occur in the Central American species. Since they live and forage on rivers, streams, and ponds, they build dens or nests on land near their foraging grounds.

CONSERVATION STATUS

Neotropical river otters are considered to be uncommon throughout their range, and are seldom observed in the wild. Reasons for their decline are intense hunting in the past for the fur market and destruction or alteration of their habitats. They are fairly intolerant of pollution. They are listed under CITES Appendix I (the highest possible risk) and under the Endangered Species Act. The status of the present populations is unknown, and research is urgently needed before this important species disappears. Isolated populations still thrive in unpolluted rivers near and within several national parks in the region, including Tortuguero National Park on the Caribbean coast of Costa Rica.

Dogs

Coyotes

and

Foxes

Family
CANIDAE

Dogs, Coyotes,

and Foxes

The canid family name derives from the word "canine," used to describe the long teeth next to the incisors. These teeth are very well developed in all species of wild dogs and are key to a quick dispatch of prey in carnivores. Wild dogs, as well as cats and other carnivores, use their canines to perforate skulls and effect rapid kills. However, not all canids are exclusively meat eaters—some depend on nonanimal foods. The coyote and the gray fox, for example, are very opportunistic and will eat birds, small mammals, reptiles, amphibians, insects, berries, and other fruits with equal relish. Their omnivorous nature makes these species particularly successful in disturbed habitats where the influence of humans has upset the presence of natural prey populations.

Canids have well-developed senses of smell and hearing which they use to track their prey, find food, and mark and interpret territorial boundaries. The intelligence and social structure of several species have been thoroughly studied. Observation of the day-to-day behaviors of domestic dogs is a great exercise in understanding canids. Many of their behaviors are ritualized, meaning that they are "hard wired," or done automatically, and performed sometimes out of context in domestic breeds. Examples of these behaviors are adaptive in natural environments but make little sense in domestic situations, such as the marking of territories, particularly moving elements of territories (like car tires), and scratching after urinating or defecating. A car from out of town was always a great source of information to our dogs, as they smelled and checked every tire for hidden messages from far away lands. After "reading" all these messages, they would answer them back by urinating on each tire in turn. In nature, territories are key to the survival of individuals and family units. Central American canids tend to hunt and forage by themselves or in family groups. Coyotes, for example, are very family oriented, while gray foxes are usually observed alone. Very little is known about the habits of the bush dog or the short-eared dog in Central America.

Vocalizations in canids are another important part of their behavioral repertoire. Coyotes use a variety of vocalizations which they teach to the younger members of the family. Barks, growls, and howls are often used in combination with body movements and other visual signals. These include tail wagging, the positioning of ears, lips, and body hair, and general postures, all of which convey meaning. In species that are highly social, such as the African wild or hunting dogs and North American wolves, hierarchies within the packs are important to their social structures. Complex behaviors help the pack to remain organized and minimize conflicts that may cause injuries.

Wild canids are very intelligent and adapt well to a variety of environmental situations, including domestication. Coyotes have learned to coexist with humans and even thrive in areas where deforestation has altered habitats. While most commonly found in grasslands and open areas, they may travel great distances to reach forests and their diverse fruits. The bush dog, rarely seen and poorly studied, seems to prefer forested areas. The gray fox, perhaps the most arboreal of all the canids, inhabits areas with trees, brush, and forest edges.

Human relationships with canids have been long and tortuous. "Man's best friend," the domestic dog (*Canis familiaris*), is believed to have been domesticated over 8,000 years ago. The dingo, the only canid found in Australia, was probably a domestic dog introduced there by early settlers. However, as close as we are to our pet dogs, most wild canids, as well as other carnivores, have suffered from human intrusion into their habitats. The never-ending war between sheep and cattle ranchers and coyotes is legendary in some countries, particularly the United States, Costa Rica, and Nicaragua, where ranching is an important source of revenue. In most cases, the problems have been greatly exaggerated. The role of canids in natural ecosystems is perhaps more important than we originally thought. For example, they contribute substantially to rodent control.

Wild canids have been exploited for their fur and for sport, although in Central America this is not a very widespread practice. Foxhunting, a common sport in North America and Britain, is practically nonexistent in the region. Wild canids are poorly protected in wildlife legislation throughout Central America.

COYOTE
(Canis latrans)

Portrait of a coyote standing in a field of grass.

The howling of coyotes on a dark night is a sound that inspires deep respect, if not fear, in the minds of most people. It must be something deeply ingrained in our collective genes, for I have never been able to hear it without feeling excitement and even alarm as some deep-core nerves make the hairs on my neck and arms stand up. But repetition leads to habituation, and after hearing them night after night in Costa Rica, we got used to them, even recognizing some of the finer nuances of coyote howling.

I was living with my wife and two young children at the Maritza Biological Field Station, on the western side of Orosí volcano in northwestern Costa Rica. We were at a place where the abandoned grasslands were replaced by thick forests that blanketed the upper reaches of the volcano. Most of the lowlands were a mixture of African jaragua (*Hyparrhenia rufa*) pastures, gallery forests, and scattered pioneer trees that were beginning to grow as cattle were being removed from the new park and the natural process of reforestation was taking hold. It would be a long process before the land was again covered with the original vegetation. An aggressive fire-control program led by the new Guanacaste National Park's administration allowed pioneer plants to thrive and replace the cattle grasses. In the meantime, the grass-covered landscape was home to a depauperate but interesting fauna, among them several species known to benefit from deforestation. Coyotes were among some of the most prominent ones, although they were also found in almost all other habitats in the park.

Every night for the last few weeks we had heard the coyotes. Sometimes they were far in the distance, and sometimes they were very near the house. Regular visitors at the station, they came to the house while we slept to "borrow" whatever items we were careless enough to leave on the porch. I regularly found chewed-up rubber boots and brooms, and once the leftovers of my camera case were strewn around the corral in front of the main house. At night, we were richly and abundantly rewarded with their eerie calls. The concert was started by the male with a low "ooooo," much like the beginning sound of a police-car siren, that increased in volume and pitch, to be followed by a high and long "aiiiiiooooouuuu" that tapered down to a hushed bark. Sometimes it would waver for a few seconds. That's when the chills and goose bumps would arrive. Almost immediately, a higher pitched, nearly identical sequence was called by the female, accompanied about halfway through with an encore by the male. The song was repeated once or twice, and then it would stop. Silence would envelop the grasslands, as if waiting for an answer that was often heard in the distance. Another coyote couple would mark their territory.

One night we were surprised by three new voices in the choir. After the initial song by the male-female duo, an incredibly funny sequence of "yips," "ows," and "yaws" piped in, breaking the spell (meaning the goose bumps went down) and bringing smiles to all of us. The couple had made a family and the new arrivals were now old enough to join their parents in nightly forays and howling. My five-year-old daughter became skilled at imitating the young coyotes, often eliciting hilarious exchanges with the coyotes.

As the dry season progressed, the pups grew to lanky replicas of their parents. We often saw them at dusk in the abandoned corrals in front of the station's main house, chasing each other or jumping on top of the prone and patient father. They bit his ears and tail while the mother lay nearby. As soon as darkness enveloped the landscape, the familiar chorus would start. We followed the lessons through the weeks, listening to the developing voices of the pups as their baby "yips" and "ows" were replaced by proper howls.

C. DE LA R.

TAXONOMY AND RELATIVES

The scientific name of the coyote, *Canis latrans*, comes from the Latin words "canis," which means dog, and "latrans," which means "that barks or howls." So the coyote is "the dog that barks or howls," which pretty much describes the species. Coyotes are closely related to wolves (*Canis lupus*), which do not extend into Central America, and domestic dogs (*Canis familiaris*), which are everywhere. Other members of the Canidae family that live in Central America are the gray fox (*Urocyon cinereoargenteus*), the bush dog (*Speothus venaticus*), and the small-eared dog (*Atelocynus microtis*). About 19 subspecies of coyotes have been described, showing variations in their size and coloration. Many of these subspecies might be simply geographical races. The species was first described by Say in 1823.

COMMON NAMES

Coyote, brush wolf; perro de monte (Mexico); as well as various indigenous names, mostly from Mexico.

DESCRIPTION

Coyotes are widely variable throughout their range, both in size and in coloration. They are about the size of a small or young German shepherd, ranging in size from 70 cm up to 1 m in length, not including an often black-tipped bushy tail that can measure 25 to 40 cm. They weigh between 8 and 13 kg. Their pelage varies from grayish-brown to yellow-brown, with darker or black

*Face of a
young coyote
panting.*

hairs interspersed in the coat. They also have lighter areas in the throat and
on the rear end. Their ears are fairly large (10 to 12 cm) and pointed, and their
face is long, with a pointed, thin muzzle. Their shuffling gait and low tail position when walking and trotting are also characteristic.

Coyotes are shy and skittish. Their tracks are longer and thinner than
those of dogs of similar size, showing longer claws and toe pads that are
closer together. These two characteristics would allow anyone to differentiate
coyote tracks from those of dogs and wolves. Also, the front track is usually
larger than the hind track.

DENTAL FORMULA

I3/3, C1/1, P4/4, M2/2, for a total of 40 teeth.

HABITAT AND DISTRIBUTION

The coyote is perhaps one of the best-studied carnivore species, although most of the research has been carried out on populations in the United States and Mexico. Originally from open areas and grasslands in the southern United States and Mexico, the coyote has expanded its range north into Canada and Alaska and south into Central America and Panama. They also have been introduced into Florida and Georgia. It is safe to say that the coyote has benefited greatly from the activities of humans in their region. Deforestation and creation of pasture land has replaced forested areas, which in turn has made available ample suitable habitat for this species. However, their presence in and use of forested areas (such as the Pacific deciduous and semideciduous dry forests of Costa Rica in the Guanacaste Province) might indicate that forested areas were not alien to this species at one time. Preferred habitats are open range and edge habitats, although we have observed them going into forests in

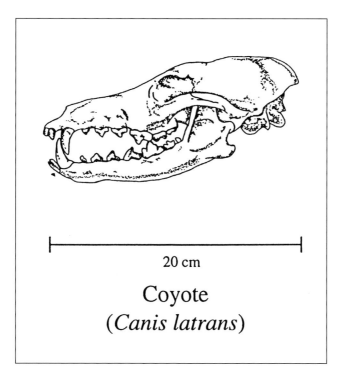

20 cm

Coyote
(*Canis latrans*)

search of fruits. The adaptability of the coyote to winter conditions in temperate regions of its range is truly amazing, particularly for a species which seems to have evolved in tropical and subtropical climates.

Home ranges can be very large, covering anywhere from 5 to 70 square kilometers, and the home ranges of one family overlap those of other families. Territories are smaller, marked with scent posts and scat, and are defended from intruding groups. Among family groups, hierarchies have been observed, with both males and females dominant.

BEHAVIOR

Coyotes are variable and adaptable in their behavior. They can be diurnal or nocturnal and feed on a wide variety of items. They are known to eat small rodents such as field mice and squirrels, and also carrion (either killed by other animals or road kills), birds, eggs, rabbits, raccoons, opossums, and insects. Whenever they encounter a large carcass (such as a dead cow, calf, or horse), they usually approach it from the rear, eating first the organs and then the flesh from the legs. They also eat fruits, other plants, and garbage. The adults regurgitate food for the pups at the den.

Coyotes are generalists and opportunists in their food habits. They have

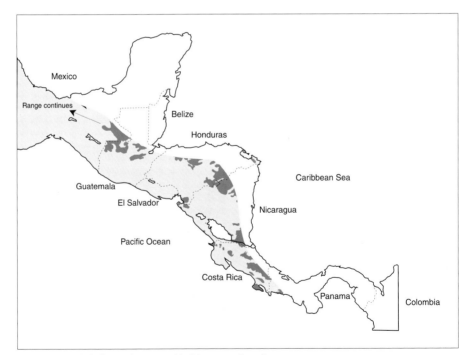

21. *Historical (light) and present (dark) coyote distribution.*

Adult coyote howling.

adapted well to disturbed habitats and to human habitation areas. Cattle pastures and garbage pits are excellent foraging places for coyotes. They can be very bold in approaching humans but are usually shy, putting safe distances between themselves and people, especially where they have been hunted or controlled. They may come into people's houses in search of food morsels and items that interest them. For example, as mentioned above, I had a leather camera case, boots, brushes, brooms, and assorted articles stolen by coyotes from the porch of our house in Guanacaste National Park. Often these items were chewed up and abandoned in a nearby pasture. Coyotes are fond of garbage and may dig small tunnels into garbage pits, chewing through ropes and tie-downs to open garbage pails. Our own observations of coyote scat in Guanacaste recorded plastic, leather, paper, and even pieces of aluminum and steel in scats found along the road. Sometimes these were several kilometers from the garbage sources.

The role of coyotes as forest seed dispersers has not yet been explored. We found abundant seeds of several species (such as *Manilkara* spp., which grow inside the forests, and *Byrsonima crassifolia*, which grows in open semideciduous forests and on open grasslands) in scats over 10 kilometers from the nearest place where these plants were found. They would often walk several kilometers into a forest to reach a particular fruiting tree and then return to their dens kilometers away.

Coyotes are easy to observe and identify. Their scat is often found on trails and dirt roads, and inspection of it can give insights into what local coyotes are eating. Again, a word of caution here: coyote and other wild animal scats often harbor parasites that can infect humans, and some even can be inhaled (see the raccoons for more details). Remember that the urine of wild mammals can contain bacteria called *Leptospires* that can be very dangerous to humans. Always use gloves and sticks to manipulate wild scats.

More people will hear coyotes than see them, and their howls have kept many people awake until the wee hours of the morning. Howling has specific social and territorial meanings, serving as locator, territory marker, and identification card for families or groups. Howls can be heard for several kilometers. Researchers have been able to recognize more than 10 distinct categories of howling; when added to various grunts, barks, growls, and whines, this makes coyotes one of the most expressive and communicative species among the carnivores.

REPRODUCTION

There have been few field studies of coyotes in Central America, and not many individuals have been kept and bred in captivity. Central American coyotes generally mate once a year, during a period from November to January. Gestation periods range from 60 to 65 days, and they give birth to from one to 10 pups. Normally, several males court one female when she comes into heat or estrus. Estrus lasts from four to 15 days. Females choose one male and normally stay with that male through consecutive litters. Both parents take care of the pups, and the male hunts and brings food to the female during birthing and whelping. Often, older siblings help bring food to the female and pups. Dens are dug or prepared on rocky ledges and brush-covered slopes with good visibility. These dens may be used year after year and can have several entrances. The parents may move the pups from one den to another if danger is perceived. Active dens usually show debris and litter (e.g., bones) at their entrances.

It has been reported that coyotes occasionally interbreed with dogs and wolves and that these hybrids are viable. These hybrids appear to inherit some of the parental care instincts of the coyotes. Coyotes are usually killed or displaced by wolves when their territories overlap.

Baby coyote's
first howls.

CONSERVATION STATUS

Coyotes have a bad reputation among certain sectors of society. Ranchers all over the Americas have persecuted them, and coyotes have shown a remarkable capacity to outsmart the attempts to control them. Because of their status as a pest species, their habits and behavior have been studied in much detail. However, when it comes to controlling them, there are still many unanswered questions. Most control methods seem to work for a while and then fail. Usually this is because some aspect of the biology of coyotes has not been taken into account.

We feel that the best control of coyotes is preventive. Improved animal husbandry, removal of carrion, proper management of garbage and waste, and close supervision of herds and calving animals will go a long way in preventing coyote depredation.

Coyotes can play a beneficial role in wild communities. Besides their assumed role in seed dispersal, they seem important in the control of rodent populations and in carrion disposal.

Their status as pests throughout most of their range confers this species little or no protection. They are actively hunted and eliminated when possible. Their range seems to be expanding in spite of all these control efforts. This is aided by the conversion of forest habitats to more open types of land use. It is quite possible that coyotes will invade South America through the Panamanian isthmus of Darien in the future, particularly if the Inter American Highway connection between Panama and Colombia is ever built. This project is considered a terrible idea by those who understand the severe ecological devastation and biological problems that such a road would cause.

GRAY FOX

(Urocyon cinereoargenteus)

It was the first gray fox I had ever encountered in Costa Rica. I was walking along a trail that followed a tall rock wall, when at a turn on the trail I stood face to face with a small house cat–sized animal. At least that is what I thought it was at first. However, in the seconds that it took us to realize what the other was, the distinct doglike face, big eyes, long ears, and half-opened, pointy muzzle identified it as a gray fox. I have seen many red foxes (*Vulpes vulpes*) and gray foxes in Pennsylvania and West Virginia, but this one was much smaller than I had expected.

Portrait of a female gray fox sitting.

The fox quickly finished its inspection of me and decided to retreat. To my amazement, it climbed straight up the nearly vertical rock wall and continued to crawl up the trunk of a tree that leaned over the edge of the 15-foot wall, disappearing into the leafy branches. At the point where it had started to climb, I found a half-eaten mouse. I had rudely interrupted its meal. Upon returning to the house, I searched in my library for information on this common but rarely seen species. I found out that indeed this species is fond of climbing trees and is uniquely adapted to this feat by having semiretractile nails. Perhaps it is this ability to avoid leaving scent trails by getting off the ground that prompted frustrated foxhunters to import from England the more earthbound red fox into America (Rezendes, 1992).

According to a fine and superbly illustrated book (although long out of print), A. Starker Leopold (1959) observed gray foxes climbing trees and hiding among the thick branches to escape chasing dogs. He also reported encountering gray foxes sunning themselves while perched on the forks of branches high in trees.

The reputation of foxes for outwitting their enemies is legendary. I once had the rare pleasure of observing a gray fox eluding a dog pack during a traditional English foxhunt. I had recently arrived at Kennett Square, a small town in southeastern Pennsylvania known for its concentration of wealth, large farms, polo tournaments, and steeple-chase horse breeders. Having just moved to a 200-year-old log cabin, I took a leisurely Saturday morning walk through the woods that surrounded the house. I followed a well-trodden trail along a stream and was completely immersed in the sights and sounds of the cold spring morning. A most foreign sound crept into my consciousness: baying hounds and the movielike sound of a bugle.

I stopped on the trail, trying to determine either the source of the sound or the nature of my most unlikely imaginings. But I was not imagining things; I could hear them coming closer and could even feel the low rumble of approaching running horses. I stepped into the bushes that lined the side of the trail in time to see a fox running full tilt along it, its tongue hanging over the side of its mouth. About 50 feet from where I was hiding, the fox jumped off the trail, ran along a fallen tree trunk, and vanished in the tangled vegetation. The baying of the hounds intensified, and soon the first ones appeared on the trail. They ran past the place where the fox had disappeared, some of them stopping and sniffing the sides of the trail, but they eventually continued on, following the leaders of the pack. I stepped back on the trail but was immediately driven back by a gaggle of horseback riders that thundered past my retreat, ducking branches and precariously clinging to and trying to maintain control over their gigantic, sweaty mounts. Flashes of red tailcoats, black

Adult gray fox looking down from a tree perch.

riding caps (with the eventual and incongruous sight of a rider wearing a black top hat), fur, and mud crossed my sight, until the bulk of the crowd had passed and the thundering subsided.

Shaking a little at having nearly been trampled, I walked out of the now too-dangerous woods and looked for an open high place from which to follow this unique spectacle. I saw hounds and riders crisscross the woods and pastures, chasing the ghost of a fox that seemed to be too smart for them. The hounds and riders passed again near my observation place. As I got ready to leave, I saw the fox trotting in the opposite direction of the chase. It passed no more that 20 feet from where I was. It looked tired and its tongue was still hanging from the side of its mouth, but I'm almost sure I saw a little twinkle in its eyes. C. DE LA R.

TAXONOMY AND RELATIVES

The gray fox is the only fox that extends its range into Central America. It was first described by Schreber in 1775, but under the genus *Canis*. The genus *Urocyon* was at that time considered by some authors a subgenus of *Vulpes* and *Canis*. This scientific name comes from the Greek words "uro," which means tail, and "kuon," which means dog. *Cinereoargenteus* comes from two Latin words, "cinereus," which means ash-colored, and "argenteus," which means silvery. Together, they mean "silvery ash-colored dog with tail," which describes this animal pretty well. Some 16 subspecies have been described, most of them in the United States.

The gray fox is closely related to the red fox (*Vulpes vulpes*), with whose geographic range its range overlaps, and with two other species that occur only in North America, the kit fox (*Vulpes macrotis*) and the swift fox (*Vulpes velox*). Other relatives from South America are the grey zorro (*Dusicyon griseus*) from Chile and Argentina, an important commercial species for its pelt, and the Azara's zorro (*Dusicyon gymnocercus*) from Paraguay, Uruguay, Brazil, and Argentina. There are seven species of foxes living in South America.

In Central America, the gray fox has probably been affected by the conversion of forested land into pastures and urban environment. However, until more research is conducted on this species, we will not be able to assess the true status of their wild populations.

COMMON NAMES

Gray fox; zorra gris, gato de monte (literally "bush cat," probably because of its ability to climb trees), zorro; gato cervan (Honduras).

DESCRIPTION

This is a relatively small mammal whose body can measure up to 75 cm in length and whose bushy tail measures between 28 and 41 cm long. Adults can weigh as little as 3 kg and as much as 6 kg. Unique among canids, gray foxes have semiretractile nails, a possible adaptation to their semi-arboreal life. When viewing their tracks, the nails do not always register as they do in all other canids, particularly the nails on the hind feet. Often, gray fox tracks are mistaken for cat tracks.

They are opportunistic feeders and thrive on a great variety of animal and plant materials. Rabbits seem to be important sources of food at all latitudes, and they are fond of fruits, mice, squirrels, rats, moles, insects, and even carrion. Their delicate teeth prevent them from crushing large bones easily. The more carnivorous their diet (and therefore bloodier), the darker the scats appear.

They have a black stripe along the back which gives the appearance of a mane, and the tip of their tail is black. Often, reddish-colored fur is present on the neck area and the sides. The throat and jaws are usually white.

Gray foxes can live up to 15 years in the wild, although in captivity they seldom live beyond 10 years.

DENTAL FORMULA

I3/3, C1/1, P4/4, M2/2, for a total of 40 teeth.

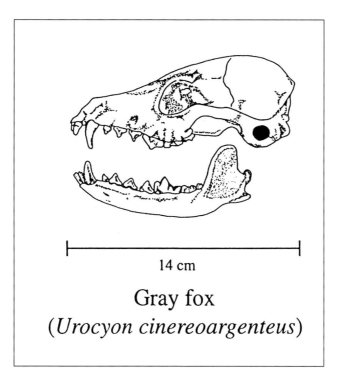

14 cm

Gray fox
(*Urocyon cinereoargenteus*)

HABITAT AND DISTRIBUTION

Gray foxes inhabit forested areas and thick brush, although they also forage near forest edges and venture into pastures and scattered brush. Their arboreal habits make them stick to areas with some woodland. Similar to many cats, gray foxes like to climb high and survey their territories from these vantage points. They are found from the U.S.-Canada border to the western United States, and south to northern Colombia and Venezuela. In Venezuela and Colombia they appear to favor mid to high elevations.

BEHAVIOR

Most of the behavioral studies of the gray fox have been conducted on North American populations, but there is no compelling reason to believe that the Central American races or populations behave much differently. The gray fox's ability to climb trees makes it unique among the canids. As described in the encounter, they can be very fast climbers and apparently spend a good part of their time resting or sleeping in trees. They can even climb telephone poles, which is amazing evidence of their climbing prowess. Foxes mark their territories by using rocks and small bushes as scent posts, depositing on them urine which has a scent that slightly resembles that of skunks, but much milder. As in other wild canids, they defecate on their walking trails and also deposit scents (from anal glands) on the scat. The smell of the scat is generally musky.

As in other canids, foxes show specific behaviors that relate to hierarchies, dominance, and other aspects of an apparently social life. However, these observations have been made only in captive animals. It is possible that in the wild, a social structure operates in family groups (male, female, pups, and perhaps older siblings). Most of the typical canid behaviors (tail tucks and other submissive behaviors; teeth baring and "grinning"; back arching; pilo-erection, or the raising of the hair on the back; and other behaviors) have been observed in captive gray foxes. It is possible that family groups maintain separate territories in the wild.

REPRODUCTION

Dens are usually found in cavities made by other animals, as well as in hollow trees, caves, rock crevices, and wood piles. The females, or vixens, also

Four facial expressions of an adult gray fox.

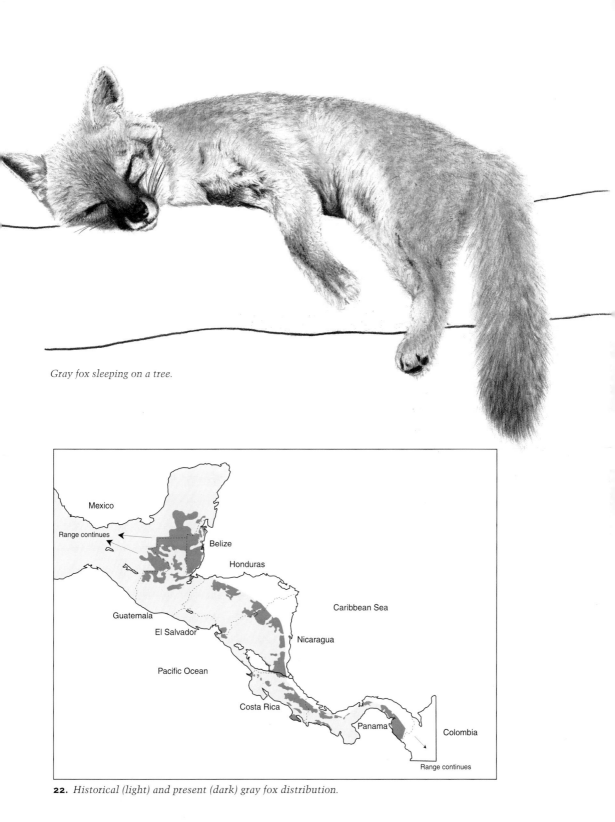

Gray fox sleeping on a tree.

22. *Historical (light) and present (dark) gray fox distribution.*

dig their own dens or modify burrows from other animals if no other
place is available. These dens can be
amazingly complex, with multiple
entrances and "rooms," or cham-
bers, used for the young and for
food storage. Food and bones are
commonly found around the entrance to the den. The gestation period has been reported anywhere
from 50 to 65 days, and they have
between three and seven pups per
litter once a year. Pups are born
blind and brown in color. They
open their eyes at about 10 days of
age. Most reproductive studies have
been made in foxes from temperate
regions, so we are not sure how much
the reproductive information can be
extrapolated to the tropical populations. There are probably differences in
the timing of their reproduction due to
the winters in the northern parts of their
range. It appears that in southern U.S.
populations, gray foxes establish strongly
bonded pairs during the rearing season. The
male collaborates in the feeding and care of
the young (Eisenberg, 1989).

*Portrait of
a baby
gray fox.*

CONSERVATION STATUS

Gray foxes, as well as other fox species, have been traditionally hunted and
trapped for their fur in the Americas. However, wild Central American populations are seldom exploited for the fur trade. Foxes are mostly killed because
of their occasional visits to poultry and other domestic animal pens. They
seem to adapt fairly well to the presence of humans and the consequent disturbed habitats. Their crepuscular and nocturnal habits allow them to live
near human settlements practically undetected.

Gray foxes are not listed in the CITES appendices for Central America, although the trade on this and other fox species is relatively high in some countries, mostly in South America.

SMALL-EARED DOG OR SHORT-EARED DOG

(Atelocynus microtis)

Portrait of a short-eared dog.

José, a native from the legendary Panamanian Emberá tribe, led the way through the close, tangled vegetation in the humid afternoon. If José was following a trail, he was the only one who could see it. It appeared that he was going ahead, cutting a branch here, trimming a vine there, following some invisible clues apparent to his eyes only. Sigi Weisel, a German biologist volunteering on a research project, followed José, opening the trail a little wider to allow for his taller and wider frame, as well as for his inability to match José's contortions as he squeezed through openings like a forest dweller. It was the summer of 1984. Sigi was working for Dr. Pepper Trail, an ornithologist from the University of California at Berkeley. He was conducting a study on a sparrow-sized forest bird native to Panama. Trail and his students collected tissue samples and recorded the bird's songs from various localities in the Darién and Chiriquí regions of Panama. The Darién is one of the most inhospitable remaining regions of Central America. Commonly referred to as the "Darién Gap," it is the only interruption to the Pan American Highway, which runs from North America to South America. The Darién, roughly five million hectares (12.5 million acres) of lowland primary rain forest, has proven impenetrable for developers because of its harsh environment and because of the bureaucracy that encircles these lands near the border with Colombia.

José followed his trail at a fast clip, in spite of the 30-kilogram backpacks they were each carrying. Sweat pooled in the small of Sigi's back as José stopped upon reaching a clearing. A clear, shallow river ran through. Sigi welcomed the break and went for a refreshing swim with José. About 10 meters from where the men were bathing, the vegetation parted and three slender, doglike animals came into view and entered the river. Two of them were already in the water when the third one caught sight of the mostly submerged men. The third animal emitted a short growl that alerted the other two in the water, and all motion stopped for a few interminable moments. The men must have presented a rather strange sight to the animals: two bobbing heads, one light-skinned and blond, the other dark-skinned and black-haired, floating in the middle of the river. To the men, the sight was no less strange. The three dog- or foxlike animals were short-legged with dark brown pelage, long snouts, and heavy teeth. The men could see their bared teeth and hear their growls. The ears were small and nearly round. By the looks of the ones in the water, they could swim well.

It occurred to Sigi that the behavior of the three animals was peculiar because they showed no fear toward them. Moreover, they seemed to be moving slowly into a broad semicircle, as if trying to encircle them, two in the water and the third maintaining its position on land.

"What are these animals, José?" Sigi whispered in Spanish to the Emberá.

"I don't know, señor Sigi," responded the Emberá, obviously puzzled by the strange creatures. In all the years tramping though these forests, José was having his first encounter with the small-eared dog. And, by the look of things, neither José nor the dogs were thrilled to meet each other. Sigi, a zoologist, noticed behaviors that made him think of African wild dogs which hunted in teams. He finally realized, not without some horror, that they were being stalked by the dogs!

Sigi stood up, water dripping over his clothes; then everything happened very fast. When José also stood, the animals intensified their growls and snaps. However, the "bobbing heads" now looked much more formidable than when they were simply floating. The two dogs in the water swam ashore while the third growled and showed his long, heavy teeth to the men. Finally, all three retreated into the forest.

Months later, the image of these forest dogs still haunted Sigi. When he finally was able to identify them, he discovered that they were not supposed to be in Panama, but were relatively common in parts of South America. For Sigi it was not only his first encounter with the small-eared dog, it was the first time that this species had been recorded outside of South America.

C. DE LA R.

Short-eared dog.

TAXONOMY AND RELATIVES

The small-eared dog was first described in 1883 by Sclater, although with a different name. The genus *Atelocynus* was redescribed and properly placed in its present taxonomic spot by Cabrera in 1940. There is still some degree of controversy over the placement of the species in either of two genera, *Dusi-cyon* (supported by recent work by Gittleman, 1996) and *Atelocynus*, found in other current tropical mammal sources (e.g., Eisenberg, 1989). The species has been called *Canis microtis* in the past, although no one uses that name anymore. It is the only species in the *Atelocynus* genus, if one follows that nomenclature. Other South American species in the *Dusicyon* genus are the hoary fox (*D. vetulus*), the crab-eating fox (*D. sechurae*), the pampas fox (*D. gymnocercus*), and the Argentine gray fox (*D. griseus*), among others. The species name *microtis* means "small ears."

COMMON NAMES

Small-eared dog, short-eared dog (United States); small-eared zorro, zorro de orejas cortas, zorro negro, zorro de monte (Spanish).

DESCRIPTION

At first impression, this dog looks like a dark-colored fox but with smaller, rounder ears and a stouter muzzle. It measures between 70 cm and 1 m at the shoulder in length, with a bushy tail between 25 and 35 cm long, which is pretty long for an animal this size. Adults can weigh up to 9 kg, making it about the size of a small domestic dog. Its coat is dark brown with white hairs peppering the dorsal parts. An area of darker hair along its midline can appear as a diffuse stripe in some animals. It walks carefully and purposefully, more like a cat than a dog. Its hazel eyes shine pale green under a light. Another interesting and prominent feature is that the robust canine teeth are visible even when the mouth is closed. They also have enlarged second molars.

DENTAL FORMULA

I3/3, C1/1, P4/4, M2/3, for a total of 42 teeth.

HABITAT AND DISTRIBUTION

Its normal range is the Amazon Basin, although it has also been recorded in southeastern and northeastern Colombia. Its presence in Panama, although previously unrecorded, is possible due to the continuous mass of forest habitat that covers the region. However, it is considered extremely rare throughout its range. It usually occurs in undisturbed primary and gallery forests in the Amazon (Brazil) and Orinoco (Venezuela) basins, and in parts of Peru, Colombia, Ecuador, and Panama.

BEHAVIOR

Very little is known about the small-eared dog in the wild. When it has been seen, it appears to move alone, or in pairs or small family groups. It also seems to be the least sociable of the dog family. Most of the behaviors mentioned here were observed in captive animals. They are mostly nocturnal or crepuscular and terrestrial, and almost nothing is known of their reproductive habits, hunting techniques, or other aspects of their natural history. In captivity, individuals do not bond strongly, communicating among themselves with a very limited vocal repertoire. When excited, the males emit a musky odor. They also growl when threatened.

REPRODUCTION

Unknown.

CONSERVATION STATUS

The small-eared dog is considered extremely rare throughout its range, although no special conservation status has been given to the species. It should probably be considered at least "vulnerable" due to the loss of its main habitat. Research on this species is badly needed; it is very difficult to assess the status of a species and to design management actions for its protection and survival if we simply don't know anything about its habits, behavior, or ecological needs.

23. *Location of single record of small-eared dog in Central America.*

*Portrait of a
bush dog.*

BUSH DOG

(Speothos venaticus)

The Osa Peninsula, in southern Costa Rica, is a beautiful, wild place. Parts of
it were established as Corcovado National Park in 1975, with other sections
added in later years. This protected status has not spared the park from conflict; a series of invasions by settlers, loggers, hunters, and later, gold miners,
periodically has disturbed the peaceful setting. In spite of its troubled history,
Osa is wild and species rich, both in plants and animals. Walking through the
seemingly undisturbed forests of the peninsula, one is awed by the size of the
trees. Some reach up to 80 meters in height. Over 280 species of birds have
been recorded, as well as 140 species of mammals, 16 freshwater fishes, and
over 100 reptiles and amphibians. Reportedly, there are sections of the park
that boast over 100 species of trees in half a hectare. However, here and there
one can find a large tree with a short stem of thick barb-wire growing through
the middle. Many areas in Osa were pastures over 100 years ago. They were
small plots carved out of the jungle that were bordered with a few lines of
wire to keep the jungle out and a few cows in. Some of these trees were once

fence posts and are now mute and hard-to-find evidence of the troubled past. The park is slowly being ringed by development and logging. In time, as has happened to many other natural areas in Central America, it will be an island of forest amidst converted agro-ecosystems.

On the northern edge of the Corcovado National Park is the Marenco Biological Field Station, a remote and roadless 500-hectare private reserve and field laboratory. It has spectacular views to the ocean and to the forest. Despite only being accessible by air or boat, it has been the site of many recent investigations. It is also where many tourists interested in animal viewing go. Pablo Riba, one of several resident biologists at Marenco, was taking a group of Italian tourists for a walk on the Rainforest Trail which leads through lush forest to the shores of the Claro River. From there, they were going to follow the Beach Trail and return to the station. Early morning is the best time to hear and see wildlife. The group carried photo and video equipment, anticipating great photo opportunities. What neither Pablo nor the tourists anticipated was what would eventually become the first sighting of the elusive bush dog in Costa Rica (another sighting was recently reported in the newsletter of the San Vito Biological Station, Organization of Tropical Studies).

Walking slowly along the narrow trail, Pablo pointed out the many interesting tidbits of natural history that make him a superb guide. In spite of his youth, his knowledge of the biology of the region is vast, and his enthusiasm about the many different plants and animals is contagious. Pablo talked in whispers to the tourists as he pointed to forest birds that seemingly only he could see in the canopy above. The eyes of the tourists were glued to the tiny screens and viewfinders of their photo and video cameras. Pablo looked down and was surprised by the appearance of two small doglike animals on the trail ahead. Cameras clicked and whirred, the tourists focusing on the canopy birds as Pablo tried to come up with a name for these animals on the ground. He had never seen them before. Quietly, he gained the attention of the nearest tourists and asked them to photograph or film the animals. The movement alerted the animals; they stopped, sniffed the air, and attempted to recognize the creatures ahead. The video cameras recorded two short, squat doglike animals as they turned around and scampered into the vegetation by the side of the trail. They left no tracks in the thick carpet of wet leaves. Only the fleeting video record allowed the startling identification weeks later.   C. DE LA R.

TAXONOMY AND RELATIVES

The genus *Speothus* was described by Lund in 1839, with the species *S. venaticus* described in 1842. Three subspecies have been reported by Wozencraft (1995).

COMMON NAMES

Bush dog, vinegar fox (English); zorro vinagre, perro de monte, perro grullero (Venezuela); perro de matorral, ictición.

DESCRIPTION

This is a sausage-shaped dog with a short snout, very small ears, and short legs and tail. Its stocky face resembles slightly the weasel's. Normally, its pelage is reddish-brown with a yellowish head and neck. The legs and tail are dark brown or even black. It attains a body length between 60 and 75 cm (not counting the tail) and a height of 23 cm (measured at the back). Its tail is between 12 and 15 cm long, and it weighs between 5 and 7 kg.

DENTAL FORMULA

I3/3, C1/1, P4/4, M1–2/2, for a total of 38 to 39 teeth. This is a unique dental formula among carnivores.

HABITAT AND DISTRIBUTION

It is commonly found in primary and gallery forests, savannas, steppes, and, less often, open forests. This is mostly a South American species, found in

Bush dog. Notice the short legs, stout body, and short tail.

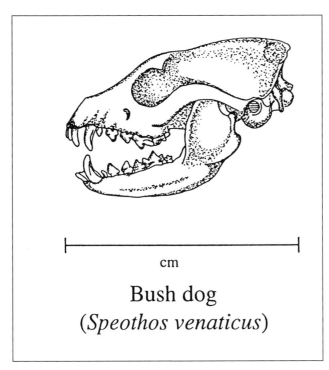

cm

Bush dog
(*Speothos venaticus*)

eastern Panama, eastern Colombia, Guyana, Brazil, Paraguay, eastern Peru, and northern Bolivia. It is reportedly rare within this large range. In Central America, it is known only from Panama and Costa Rica.

BEHAVIOR

Bush dogs are exclusively carnivorous. They hunt in packs of up to 10 animals and may attack larger animals, such as tapirs, which they follow into the water. They are good swimmers and divers. They are also good diggers and are fond of using and modifying the dens of other animals, such as armadillos. They also hunt capybaras and rheas (in South America), agoutis, and other small mammals, such as rodents and invertebrates.

Both males and females mark territories using urine and other glandular secretions. The males lift their rear legs 90 degrees just like domestic dogs do. The females have a most peculiar way of marking. They raise themselves on the front legs, seeking support on a tree or on the object they are marking, urinate, and then slide their legs down. Other forms of communication include sounds such as frequent whines, short barks, grunts, whispers, and

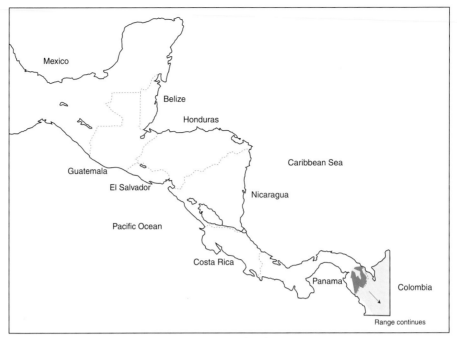

Mexico

Belize

Honduras

Guatemala

El Salvador

Nicaragua

Caribbean Sea

Pacific Ocean

Costa Rica

Panama

Colombia

Range continues

24. *Historical (light) and present (dark) bush dog distribution.*

howls. There is a strong pair bond between mated males and females, and packs are fairly cohesive. The males reportedly feed the nursing females, and pups share their food as well. They seem to be aggressive in their encounters with other animals and humans, although some Brazilian indigenous tribes have been able to domesticate or tame them. Most behavioral observations have been made of captive packs, as there are very few studies or accounts of observations in the field.

REPRODUCTION
Bush dogs are believed to have at least two litters per year, consisting of three to six pups each. Gestation lasts about 65 days. The young stay with the parents for several months, and they do not reproduce until they leave their parents.

CONSERVATION STATUS
Although they have been studied very little, they are listed as "vulnerable" by IUCN. Because they are rare, we know very little of their natural history. Apparently, they are not persecuted by humans throughout most of their range. Their "vulnerable" status and their possible decline in numbers most probably is due to the disappearance of their habitat. The species is protected in Peru and in Brazil, and it is listed in IUCN's Red List and in CITES Appendix I.

Baby bush dog.

The Future of

Carnivores

Central American

Conservation Issues

The animals presented in these pages are, in general, well-recognized denizens of tropical forests and other Central American wildlands. Many are attractive and have a certain degree of charisma that makes them interesting to people. One of the main motivations for writing this book was to compile and share the current knowledge about Central American carnivores, because the more people know about carnivores and the ecosystems they live in, the better we'll be able to come up with ways and resources to manage and conserve their populations into perpetuity.

Carnivores, as top members of food webs in the tropics, to a great degree depend on the continuity in structure and function of their home ecosystems, and they play an important role in maintaining the balance of these natural ecosystems. Thus, a discussion about the conservation of carnivores in the tropics is also a discussion about conservation of whole ecosystems, and herein lies the crux of the conservation issue in this region. We need to look at these species as integral and functional parts of a large machine that needs every piece to run smoothly and continuously. And these machines are embedded within complex assemblages which have nearly been wiped out in many parts of the region.

In this chapter we'll talk about specific issues that concern the conservation of carnivores in Central America, with the understanding that this also implies knowing, conserving, and managing whole ecosystems. Many of the following observations can be extrapolated to other developing tropical areas of the world as well. The basic lesson here is that we cannot protect a species or group of species outside of their environmental context. The conservation of tropical carnivores will require a careful plan and a series of actions that are geared toward the protection of entire ecosystems. This does not mean, as we will see, that we should not be continuing or even increasing the implementation of programs designed to protect single species or groups of species (wild cats, for example). Ex-situ conservation, as it is called, has an important role to play in conservation. However, both approaches should be accomplished simultaneously and in coordination if we are to succeed in the preservation of healthy populations of these species.

"EXTINCT IS FOREVER; ENDANGERED MEANS THERE'S STILL TIME"

What does it mean to be endangered? Throughout this book, we frequently refer to species as being endangered or threatened with extinction. In this section, we define what it means to be endangered and describe the situation of carnivores in general in the region.

The IUCN (International Union for the Conservation of Nature) produces a variety of publications that examine the status and the latest research findings on many species of plants and animals. They define endangered this way:

> Endangered: Taxa in danger of extinction and whose survival is unlikely if the causal factors continue operating. Included are taxa whose numbers have been reduced to a critical level or whose habitats have been so drastically reduced that they are deemed to be in immediate danger of extinction. Also included are taxa that may be extinct but have definitely been seen in the wild in the past 50 years. (from the IUCN website, www.iucn.org)

Endangered means a species is about to disappear from the face of the earth, or to become extinct. There is no return from the state of extinction, at least not with the present or foreseeable future state of genetic engineering and DNA replication. The genetic manipulation portrayed in Jurassic Park is hypothetical, not reality; we are many years away, if ever, from achieving the ability to resurrect extinct species with salvaged DNA samples. Many species of plants and animals have already become extinct. The dodo and the passenger pigeon are examples of contemporary extinct species, as are the thousands of other species (like the dinosaurs) throughout the last 65 million years of the history of the earth.

It has been estimated than over 100 species become extinct *every day*. By the year 2000, the number of species lost *each year* could climb as high as 40,000. This is a higher rate of extinction than the greatest extinctions of the past 65 million years combined. And this new wave of massive extinctions is all caused by humans. One may ask the question, "Does it really matter that so many species are becoming extinct?"

Frequently we hear that the present extinctions are comparable to the massive extinctions of the past, like during the Cretaceous period when dinosaurs became extinct. As Janzen (1997) and other authors point out, there are some very important differences between the Cretaceous and other past waves of extinctions and the one we are causing now. For example:

1. Evolution works on the materials available, meaning the available pool of species and their populations. At the present rate of losses, there is not going to be much material for evolution to work on in the future. Moreover, the present rate of extinction is not favoring some groups (such as mammals or reptiles) over others, but treating everything from carnivores to fungi equally. The great radiation of placental mammals in the Cretaceous ultimately gave origin to humans. The evolution and diversification of other groups of reptiles, birds, insects, and amphibians that survived the Cretaceous will likely not occur after this wave of extinction is over.

2. Not only are we eliminating species, but we are also eliminating whole types of environments, basically homogenizing the land. And the environments that are disappearing at the highest rates are those that have the greatest number of species: tropical forests, wetlands, and coral reefs.

3. Rather than having an enormous potential for the development of new life forms to colonize ecological niches left by the extinct groups of species, we'll have the equivalent of many thousands of small islands of habitat where species will become endemic. Most of the available niches (urban and various forms of agro-ecosystems) will be occupied already by highly adaptable species that often tend to become nuisances to humans.

4. Whatever species survive the present wave of extinction will not be determined by their ability to overcome certain global change in their environment, but by the serendipitous selection of areas that are spared destruction and by the size of these areas.

In the best of cases, whether we continue to eradicate ecosystems at the present rate or even if we stop the mass deforestation in the tropics, we face the loss of some 10 to 20% of all living species of plants and animals that presently live on the planet. The number could become higher if we do not act to change some of the directions that international conservation efforts are leading us. Unfortunately, many of these species are going to disappear without us even knowing them, what roles they play in ecosystems, or what possible benefits they could have for humans.

Scientists have described, identified, and cataloged more than one-and-a-half million species of plants and animals, but they estimate that there could be up to 20 to 40 million species on earth. This means that we still have many more species to discover and to describe than the ones we already know. Some groups of plants and animals are much better known than others; it is unlikely that we are going to find many new species of large mammals, birds, reptiles, amphibians, or fishes, although once in a while new ones do appear. On the other hand, the number of unknown species of insects, fungi, mites, and other groups is much larger than those we already know. Working on aquatic insects in Costa Rica, one of the authors (C. de la R.) and his colleagues have discovered over 400 species of aquatic insects new to science in only a few years, all within the 50,900 square kilometers of this little Central American country. This number is likely to double in the next few years. The process of studying, describing, assigning names to, and cataloging such large numbers could take several lifetimes of work for taxonomists.

Is there time? For some species, no, there isn't. They will be gone forever. There is time for the species we include in this book, but the time is now, today. Every species lost is irreplaceable.

WHY ARE SO MANY SPECIES ENDANGERED, THREATENED, OR BECOMING EXTINCT?

There are many reasons for the threatened or endangered status of these species, and most of them, as we described in the text, are threatened by one or more factors. We can summarize the main factors that are driving modern extinction not only of carnivores, but also of many of the species that are directly or indirectly related to them.

HABITAT LOSS

This is perhaps the worst problem carnivores and many other species face in Central America. Most countries in the isthmus have lost from 70 to nearly 100% of their natural habitats to deforestation. In some areas, deforestation has wiped out entire forests, leaving nothing behind. In other areas, deforestation has caused the severe fragmentation of habitats. In many logging operations or farming settlement processes, patches of forests are left standing because they are difficult to access or because they are set aside for future harvest. Some of these patches are purchased by conservation organizations or by governments to designate as parks and preserves. Many of today's Central American protected areas have been identified and later acquired by this "lucky find" strategy. As a result, the great majority of these isolated patches are insufficient to maintain viable populations of many animals and plants. Larger carnivores need large territories and available prey, so they are particularly affected by this fragmentation of habitats. For many species, particularly the largest ones, fragmentation means eventual local extirpation (disappearance from a given region).

The question is, how big a patch is needed to maintain viable populations of all carnivores in a region? The size of the patch needed to sustain indefinitely a breeding and stable population of a given species really depends on the particular biological and ecological characteristics of each species. These are characteristics that we either don't know at all or know only superficially. For example, we know that jaguars require large territories to survive; in some cases they need in excess of 25 square kilometers for a single individual (although there is very little published data to make definite conclusions). If we use the most widely accepted general guideline of 500 individuals as a minimum number to maintain a healthy and viable contiguous population (Robinson and Redford, 1991), we would need at least some 12,500 square kilometers of interconnected habitat for jaguars in order to assure their continued existence. This is an area of roughly 110 kilometers by 110 kilometers (or 70 miles by 70 miles). There are very few protected areas in Central America that are this large (see below). Does this mean that jaguars are doomed to disappear from the region? The answer is probably yes, at least from most of the region, although this may not happen as rapidly as we might think. Populations smaller than the theoretical viable minimum can survive for many years. However, in time, inbreeding and other genetic problems would cause the population to lose much of its genetic variability. This would rob the population of the necessary flexibility to adapt to changes in its environment. We have seen the effects of inbreeding on small populations in the Florida panther (*Puma concolor coryi*) and the African cheetah (*Acinonyx jubatus*).

OVER-HARVEST OR OVER-HUNTING

The Convention on International Trade of Endangered Species, or C.I.T.E.S. (pronounced sigh-tease), has been in the last few years one of the most important instruments in the control and reduction of the international trade in endangered species. However, CITES cannot—and does not—replace internal protection laws or measures within the countries that subscribe to it. In fact, it has little power when it comes to protecting species inside specific countries. Central American countries, because of their developing economies, still maintain high rates of overuse of resources, wildlife included.

Changes in wildlife legislation throughout the region have occurred mostly in the last two decades. These changes, however, have not been accompanied in most cases by strong and effective enforcement practices or by broad educational campaigns. These are necessary to change people's minds about traditional or culturally acceptable uses of wildlife. Hunting, for example, has been deeply ingrained in Latin American societies for centuries. Initially it was used as means of subsistence and defense against "the elements." Later it became a "manly" sport. Within our generation, we can still find people who remember the "great jaguar hunts" of less than 20 years ago. One person we interviewed told us of killing over 15 jaguars in one year in northern Costa Rica. He still has some of the trophies proudly displayed in his ranch house. Some areas in Central America still boast large tracts of relatively intact wild habitats. These protected areas are consistently visited by hunters (sports and subsistence) in spite of current legislation. In the Indio-Maíz Biological Reserve, in Nicaragua, organized large-mammal hunts are still occurring although they are illegal.

The result is that many species, especially those that can provide trophies (such as felids and canids) or usable and marketable skins (some mustelids, cats, and procyonids) are still actively hunted. They feed a healthy internal black market for by-products (skins, heads, teeth, or other parts).

Another reason for the continued hunting pressure on carnivores is a consequence of the reduction of their natural habitats and the elimination of their natural prey. This is particularly important for the large carnivores. Their normal prey includes species also heavily hunted by humans. Deer, wild pigs, agoutis and their relatives, tapirs, many birds, and even monkeys are hunted for food in many recently settled rural areas. Without their prey, carnivores begin utilizing domestic animals. Humans are not only the main predator of carnivores, but also their main competitor and habitat destroyer.

The combination of destruction of habitats and overexploitation is enough to drive most species of carnivores to extinction or extirpation. However, there are other more hidden dangers, such as pollution and its effect on top predators. For example, the bio-accumulation of pesticides and other dangerous chemicals can reduce populations significantly.

PROTECTED AREAS OF CENTRAL AMERICA

Central America, because of its land-bridge character, has been blessed by a great variety of ecosystems and life zones. There are numerous types of ecosystems: semi-arid zones along the Pacific coast, deciduous and semideciduous dry forests, rain forests, montane forests, cloud forests, beaches and mangrove forests, rivers and streams, and others. Most of the ecosystems are currently fragmented into many small pieces and the majority are unconnected. They are islands in a sea of agricultural and urban landscapes. Human activities in Central America have successfully removed more than 80% of all natural wildlands. The land has been transformed into a patchwork of usually poorly managed agricultural areas, pastures, and extensive monocultures. Among the most common patterns of land use are subsistence agriculture, in which natural wildlands are first cleared of their natural cover (trees, which are either sold to lumber companies or burned on site) and then converted to the farming of basic grains and vegetable gardens, and to pastures using traditional low-tech agricultural practices. These usually are not very environmentally friendly.

The total percent of the earth's land mass that is under some kind of protection status is about 3% (about 5 million square kilometers, encompassing all types of natural ecosystems). Many of the more than 3,500 protected areas worldwide are insufficient and inadequate to effectively protect the flora and fauna within their boundaries. This situation is exacerbated in Central America because of the difficult social and economic situations of most—if not all—of the countries of the isthmus.

There are about 200 protected areas in Central America, the majority of them smaller in size than a few square kilometers. In spite of protecting sizable representations of natural habitats, for certain species this surface area is simply not enough to maintain healthy and viable populations. Many of these protected areas lack the minimum infrastructure, personnel, and resources to effectively carry out their protection goals. In reality, some of these areas are in as much danger of disappearing due to agricultural encroachment and other wholesale disturbances as are areas with no legal protection at all.

CONSERVATION STRATEGIES FOR CARNIVORES

The perception that the general population has about the state of biodiversity and the environment in Central America is that it is being degraded to some degree, whether you ask a farmer in a rural area of Nicaragua or an educated person in an urban setting. Rural people often talk to us about "the way it used to be," usually referring to how many fish there were in a given river, or how abundant the fauna was in a particular patch of forest. And it really doesn't take a keen sense of observation to notice deforestation, gross pollution, and the general disappearance of wild lands. However, the great majority of people simply do not know what to do to stop the degradation and, in many cases, they unknowingly contribute to the process.

There is a growing conservation movement in Central America that is fed from within as well as from the outside. The influence of developed countries, particularly through motivated, charismatic conservationists, powerful international conservation NGOs (Non-Government Organizations), and development aid agencies that have adopted the environmental cause (such as the United Nations, the Organization of American States, U.S. and Canadian Agencies for International Development, and many others), has made substantial contributions to the development of conservation as a science, as a movement, and as a career in Central American countries. The region's countries have responded with increasingly complex and comprehensive legislation, as well as with conservation measures to protect species and ecosystems and protected areas. These efforts can be summarized in the following strategies:

1. Species protection. Most countries in the region possess legislation that protects individual species. In general, Central America has followed closely the development of CITES guidelines and most countries subscribe to the convention; also, most countries follow the guidelines proposed by the IUCN and other world conservation organizations for individual species or groups of species. However, wildlife legislation requires implementation and regulation, which in turn implies assigning resources (financial and human) to the protection of these species. This is where Central American countries fail, because their developing economies and recent history of internal and external social and armed conflicts have sapped their resources and estab-

lished other priorities. Humans always come first in any development and rehabilitation program, so wildlife and wildlands will continue to be a lower
priority in any developing country.

In addition, most of the available legislation protects large and showy species (carnivores included), which depend for their survival on less showy and
almost always unprotected species. Another limitation is that while the laws
protect the species against hunting, trapping, and the commercialization of
its products, little is said about the destruction, fragmentation, or alteration
of their habitats, which, as we now know, are more deleterious for the survival of the species than hunting. In most of Central America, you can get
stiffly fined if you kill a jaguar, but you can clear-cut a whole forest almost
with impunity and even, in many places, with the help of government programs. This in turn eliminates the jaguars and all other animals and plants
that occupied this space.

Legislation intended to protect single species is helpful, but only if it is
not the only or the most important element in a given conservation program.

2. Conservation of land. The creation of protected areas (national parks,
wildlife refuges, etc.) is a relatively recent historical phenomenon in Central
America. Costa Rica, the most advanced country in the region in conservation matters, decreed its first national park (Santa Rosa) in 1971. It was created originally as a Historical Monument. Since then, almost 25% of the territory in Costa Rica has come under some type of conservation management
category. However, protected areas in Central America suffer from many of

25. *Protected areas of Central America.*

the same problems and defects as their North American counterparts, among them insufficient numbers and sizes, disturbances and damages done to the areas prior to their designation, uses of the area that are incompatible with the conservation of their biodiversity, insufficient or nonexistent buffer zones around the areas, and insufficient financial and personnel resources allocated to the areas.

3. Wildlife and resource management. Even before there was wildlife conservation, there was wildlife management, its main intention being—and still is—to provide tools and guidelines for continued and sustained use of wildlife by humans. In some cases in Central America, as in the United States, wildlife managers have contributed to the conservation of species and biodiversity by recognizing the importance of habitat and ecosystem stability in the maintenance of viable and healthy populations of game species. In Central America, wildlife management, particularly of carnivores, is severely handicapped by an almost complete lack of knowledge of the most basic biology of many species. We cannot manage what we do not know, and this research is fairly low in the priorities of many countries. It is also often a low priority in the government and nongovernment institutions (such as the ministries of natural resources, universities, and NGOs) whose main role is the protection and conservation of these species.

4. Captive breeding and wildlife rescue centers. In the last few years there has been a proliferation of wildlife rescue centers in Costa Rica, as a result of the growing ecotourism industry and the willingness of tourists to shell out money to see exotic animals in cages. Some of these centers are nothing more than poorly managed minizoos, and their effect on conservation is negligible or even deleterious. Another irony of wildlife rehabilitation centers is that they often compete for donations of money that could otherwise be used to preserve habitat for all species in perpetuity. However, rescue and breeding centers, with trained professional personnel, are necessary to maintain and preserve some of the genetic material that falls in the hands of wildlife protectors. For species whose populations dwindle to numbers below the minimum 500, captive breeding and keeping might provide important individuals to a recovering population.

The issue of wildlife breeding is complex, and a thorough treatment is beyond the scope of this book. Suffice it to say that zoos and captive breeding and rescue centers can play an important role in the conservation of endangered species, but only if they go hand in hand with habitat preservation and restoration. Conservation gains very little by having species exclusively confined to cages in zoos and wildlife centers.

CITES AND OTHER INTERNATIONAL REGULATIONS AND LOCAL LEGISLATION

CITES was created as an international mechanism to monitor and protect species of special concern (those species endangered, threatened, or whose status is not fully known). It is an international agreement that countries sign, agreeing to uphold the recommendations and guidelines of the convention. As stated above, CITES provides guidelines and supports studies, but does not provide resources to protect the species that the treaty covers.

The current version of CITES was signed in Washington in 1973 and amended in Bonn, Germany, in 1979. Periodic updates are published and include species found to deserve protection or specific status, incorporating them into what is known as the Appendices. Quotes from the Appendices below are from the IUCN website cited above.

Appendix I includes ". . . all species threatened with extinction which are or may be affected by trade. Trade in specimens of these species must be subject to particularly strict regulation in order not to endanger further their survival and must only be authorized in exceptional circumstances."

Appendix II includes ". . . all species which although not necessarily now threatened with extinction may become so unless trade in specimens of such species is subject to strict regulation in order to avoid utilization incompatible with their survival; and other species which must be subject to regulation in order that trade in specimens of certain species . . . may be brought under effective control."

Finally, Appendix III includes ". . . all species which any Party (countries) identifies as being subject to regulation within its jurisdiction for the purpose of preventing or restricting exploitation, and as needing the cooperation of other Parties in the control of trade."

As can be seen, the treaty regulates and prohibits trade between the countries in the species included in the Appendices, but it says little about the types of trade or consumptive activities that occur within the countries.

CENTRAL AMERICAN CARNIVORES LISTED IN APPENDICES I AND II:

Canidae	*Leopardus pardalis*
Speothos venaticus	*Leopardus tigrinus*
Mustelidae	*Leopardus wiedii*
Lontra longicaudis	*Panthera onca*
Felidae	*Puma concolor costaricensis*
Herpailurus yaguarondi	*Puma concolor cougar*

CENTRAL AMERICAN CARNIVORES LISTED IN APPENDIX III:

Procyonidae
Bassaricyon gabbii (Costa Rica)
Bassariscus sumichrasti (Costa Rica)
Nasua narica (Honduras)
Potos flavus (Honduras)
Mustelidae
Eira barbara (Honduras)
Galictis vittata (Costa Rica)

WHAT CAN YOU DO TO PROTECT CENTRAL AMERICAN CARNIVORES?

The following are some general recommendations for people in North and Central America who would like to contribute toward the conservation of carnivores.

- Become familiar with the local and international laws that regulate the use of wildlife. Don't buy or support trade in animals or products, including pets, skins, or manufactured products that include skins or bones.
- Visit conservation projects in Central America, particularly national parks, reserves, and wildlife centers. The fees you pay to gain access to these sites are used to improve the programs and increase their effectiveness. Some of these places accept volunteers who sign up through one of several international volunteer organizations, such as Peace Corps, Green Arrow, and others.
- Become active in one of the several conservation organizations that have memberships and programs in Central America. The World Wildlife Fund, Conservation International, Earthwatch, The Nature Conservancy International, and others all have specific programs that assist Central American countries in their conservation efforts. Many of these organizations have web pages with information on memberships, programs and projects.

A FEW FINAL WORDS

"We are currently at a crossroads in tropical wildland conservation" (Janzen, 1997). Either we continue to allocate wildland for conservation at the current pace and with the current criteria, risking losing the vast majority of ecosystems and the species they contain, or we increase the effort to learn more about this biodiversity and what it needs to continue to exist, so that we can aim our conservation strategies at conserving a greater portion of it by using it in a sustainable, nondestructive manner.

For Central American carnivores, this means that we must increase research of these species in order to be able to make appropriate decisions with respect to their future management and conservation. It also means that we must continue to support and develop nondestructive uses of these species, and for Central America, this translates to ecotourism and related activities (for example, facilitated research, education, and scientific tourism, among others). We must understand that the responsibility for the disappearance or the conservation of Central American carnivores—as well as other species and their ecosystems—falls not only in the hands of the governments of the countries of the region, but also on the conservation organizations, the biologists and researchers that work in the region, and the citizens of the countries where the wildlife resides. The responsibility is a shared one between developed and developing countries. Our actions, particularly those concerning international economic exchanges in their various forms (tourism, trade, joint research, etc.), have an effect on the direction conservation takes. Conservation in Central America is an economic issue, although too often we treat it as an emotional one. For tropical conservation to succeed, it must become an economic force as powerful as agricultural exports, industry, or other economic endeavors.

The most important challenge tropical conservation is facing now is to learn how to incorporate tropical wildlands into the mainstream economies of the countries where they exist. If maintaining biodiversity in all of its complexity does not become an integral part of society—just as the arts, education, technology, agriculture, and infrastructure are—then there will be no hope of society coming up with the resources to manage it and to use it sustainably. This will mean the disappearance, forever, of many species and their ecosystems. And the world at large will be poorer because of it.

GLOSSARY

ABIOTIC devoid of life, nonliving (see biotic).

ADAPTATION a behavior, physical feature, or other characteristic that helps an animal or plant survive and make the most of its habitat. For example, the margay (*Leopardus wiedii*) can rotate its ankles to a large angle. This is an adaptation that allows it to hunt efficiently in trees.

BIOLOGICAL DIVERSITY the diversity of life on earth, reflected in the number and variety of species and populations, and the communities that they form.

BIOTIC that which has to do with living organisms.

CANOPY the upper layer of a forest.

COEVOLUTION evolutionary interaction of two or more species acting as selection pressures on each other. For example, predators and prey coevolve together.

COMMUNITY group of interacting plants and animals living in the same geographic area.

ECOSYSTEM the total interacting living (plants, animals, microbes, etc.) and nonliving (soil, water, minerals, nutrients, air, etc.) elements in a given area.

ENDANGERED SPECIES a species that is in immediate danger of becoming extinct. The jaguar is an endangered species.

EXTINCT   no longer living. The saber-toothed cat is an extinct species.

EXTIRPATION   loss of a species from a particular region or country. Such a species still exists elsewhere.

FRUGIVORE   an animal that eats primarily fruits.

GALLERY FOREST   type of forest that grows along a stream or river and its floodplain.

HABITAT   the area where an animal or plant lives and finds nutrients, water, shelter, and living space.

HERBIVORE   an animal that eats only plant material (such as a deer or cow).

INTRODUCED SPECIES   an animal or plant species that has been brought into areas where the species never lived before. Introduced species, also called exotics, often compete with and cause problems for native species.

LIFE ZONE   a recognizable type of vegetation or vegetation association defined by specific conditions of precipitation, temperature, and elevation.

MARKET HUNTING   the hunting or trapping of animals to sell for profit. For example, spotted cats were hunted commercially for their hides, which were shipped to the United States and Europe for the clothing industry.

MONTANE FOREST   type of forests associated with mountains.

NATIVE SPECIES   species that occur naturally in an area.

NATURAL SELECTION   the principal mechanisms of evolutionary change in a species. When genetic characteristics are particularly well suited for a given environment, they are passed on in higher proportions to the next generation, because they give an advantage or survival value to the individuals that possess them. This allows them also to reproduce more than individuals with poor survival adaptations.

NEOTROPICS   term given to the region comprised of parts of Mexico, Central America, and South America.

NGO   a non-governmental organization like The Nature Conservancy that works with governmental agencies to achieve goals of mutual interest.

PARAMO   type of low and scrubby vegetation found in high elevations in the Andes and in some parts of Central America.

POACH   to hunt, kill, or collect a plant or animal illegally.

POPULATION   an interbreeding group of animals or plants of the same species that lives in the same area.

PREHENSILE   type of tail of some carnivores and other animals that functions as an extra limb.

RAIN FOREST   a very wet type of forest formation, where seasonal changes are minimal or nonexistent.

RARE SPECIES species that has a small number of individuals and/or has a limited distribution. A rare species may or may not be endangered or threatened. The tiger cat (*Leopardus tigrinus*) and the bush dog (*Speothos venaticus*) are rare species.

SELECTIVE PRESSURE forces from the environment (biotic or abiotic) that influence the survivability of an organism.

TAXON *(plural taxa)* group of organisms that belong to the same evolutionary group. Mammals, for example, are a taxon (at the Class level). Genera and species are also taxa.

TAXONOMY science of the classification of organisms.

THREATENED SPECIES a species whose numbers are low or declining. A threatened species is not necessarily in immediate danger of extinction, but it is likely to become endangered if it isn't protected. The jaguarundi (*Herpailurus yaguarondi*) is threatened throughout much of its range.

LITERATURE CITED

Anderson, R., 1985. *Guide to Florida: Mammals.* Altamonte Springs, Fla.: Winner Enterprises. 56 pp.

Boza, M. A., 1994. *Biodiversidad y desarrollo en Mesoamérica: Una propuesta para contribuir con el desarrollo sostenible de Mesoamérica mediante la conservación de las especies y las áreas silvestres.* San José, Costa Rica: Proyecto Paseo Pantera, Proyecto COSEFORMA/GTZ (Cooperación en los sectores forestal y maderero). 240 pp.

Burt, W. H., and R. P. Grossenheider, 1976. *A Field Guide to the Mammals of America North of Mexico.* Boston: Houghton Mifflin Company. 289 pp.

Caire, W., J. D. Tyler, B. P. Glass, and M. A. Mares, 1989. *Mammals of Oklahoma.* Norman: University of Oklahoma Press. 567 pp.

Carrillo, E., and C. S. Vaughan (eds.), 1994. *La vida silvestre de Mesoamerica: Diagnóstico y estrategia para su conservación.* Heredia, Costa Rica: Universidad Nacional. 360 pp.

Caughley, G., and A. Gunn, 1996. *Conservation Biology in Theory and Practice.* Cambridge, Mass.: Blackwell Science. 459 pp.

Ceballos, G., and C. Galindo (eds.), 1984. *Mamíferos silvestres de la cuenca de México.* Mexico City: Limusa.

Charles-Dominique, P., M. Atramentowicz, M. Charles-Dominique, H. Gerard,

A. Hladik, C. M. Hladik, and M. F. Prevost, 1981. Les mammiferes frugivores arboricoles nocturnes d'une foret guyanaise: Inter-relations plantes. *Revue d'Ecologie (Terre et Vie)* 35: 341–435.

Eisenberg, J. F., 1989. *Mammals of the Neotropics, Vol. 1: The Northern Neotropics.* Chicago: University of Chicago Press. 449 pp.

Emmons, L. H., 1990. *Neotropical Rainforest Mammals: A Field Guide.* Chicago: University of Chicago Press. 281 pp.

———, 1997. *Neotropical Rainforest Mammals: A Field Guide,* 2nd ed. Chicago: University of Chicago Press. 307 pp.

Ewer, R. F., 1973. *The Carnivores.* Ithaca: Cornell University Press. 494 pp.

Farrand, J., Jr. (ed.), 1995. *Familiar Mammals of North America.* National Audubon Society. New York: Chanticleer Press, Inc. 190 pp.

Foster-Turley, P., S. Macdonald, C. Mason, and the IUCN/SSC (The World Conservation Union/Species Survival Commission) Otter Specialist Group, 1990. *Otters: An Action Plan for Their Conservation.* London: IUCN/SSC Otter Specialist Group. 126 pp.

Fox, M. W., 1971. *Behaviour of Wolves, Dogs and Related Canids.* Malabar, Fla.: Krieger Publishing Company. 220 pp.

Gardner, A. L., 1971. Notes on the Little Spotted Cat, *Felis tigrina oncilla* Thomas, in Costa Rica. *Journal of Mammalogy* 52: 464–465.

Ginsberg, J. R., D. W. Macdonald, and the IUCN/SSC Canid and Wolf Specialist Groups, 1990. *Foxes, Wolves, Jackals and Dogs: An Action Plan for the Conservation of Canids.* London: IUCN/SSC Canid and Wolf Specialist Groups. 116 pp.

Gittleman, J. L. (ed.), 1989. *Carnivore Behavior, Ecology and Evolution,* vol. 1. Ithaca: Cornell University Press. 620 pp.

———, 1996. *Carnivore Behavior, Ecology and Evolution,* vol. 2. Ithaca: Cornell University Press. 644 pp.

Glaston, A. R., 1994. *The Red Panda, Olingos, Coatis, Raccoons, and Their Relatives: Status Survey and Conservation Action Plan for Procyonids and Ailurids.* Gland, Switzerland: IUCN. 101 pp.

Gomes de Oliveira, T., 1994. *Neotropical Cats, Ecology and Conservation.* São Luis, Brazil: Universidade do Maranhão. 220 pp.

Gremone, C., F. Cervigón, S. Gorzula, G. Medina, and D. Novoa, 1985. *Fauna de Venezuela: Vertebrados.* Caracas, Venezuela: Editorial Biosfera. 320 pp.

Grzimek, B. (ed.), 1975. *Grzimek's Animal Life Encyclopedia: Mammals,* vols. 1 to 4. New York: Van Nostrand Reinhold. 750 pp.

Hanson, J. K., and D. Morrison, 1992. *Of Kinkajous, Capybaras, Horned Beetles, Seladangs, and the Oddest and Most Wonderful Mammals, Insects, Birds, and Plants of Our World.* New York: Harper Perennial. 285 pp.

Hoogesteijn, R., and E. Mondolfi, 1992. *El jaguar, tigre Americano.* Caracas, Venezuela: Armitano Editores C.A. 182 pp.

Janzen, D. H., 1983. *Costa Rican Natural History.* Chicago: University of Chicago Press. 816 pp.

———, 1997. Wildland Biodiversity in the Tropics, pp. 411–431. In: M. L. Reaka-Kudla, D. E. Wilson, and E. O. Wilson (eds.), 1997. *Biodiversity II: Understanding and Protecting Our Biological Resources.* Washington, D.C.: Joseph Henry Press. 551 pp.

Kaufmann, J. H., 1983. *Nasua narica* (Pizote, Coatí). In: D. H. Janzen, 1983. *Costa Rican Natural History.* Chicago: University of Chicago Press. 816 pp.

Kitchener, A., 1991. *The Natural History of the Wild Cats.* Ithaca: Comstock Publishing Associates, Cornell University Press. 279 pp.

Koford, C. B., 1983. *Felis wiedii* (Tigrillo, Caucel, Margay). In: D. H. Janzen, 1983. *Costa Rican Natural History.* Chicago: University of Chicago Press. 816 pp.

Kricher, J. C., 1989. *A Neotropical Companion: An Introduction to the Animals, Plants, and Ecosystems of the New World Tropics.* Princeton: Princeton University Press. 436 pp.

Leopold, A. S., 1959. *Fauna silvestre de Mexico.* Mexico, D.F.: Instituto Mexicano de Recursos Naturales Renovables. 641 pp.

Macdonald, D. (ed.), 1984. *The Encyclopedia of Mammals.* New York: Facts on File, Inc. 895 pp.

———, 1992. *The Velvet Claw: A Natural History of the Carnivores.* London: BBC Books. 256 pp.

Mallory, K., 1992. *Water Hole: Life in a Rescued Tropical Forest.* New York: Franklin Watts. 57 pp.

Marineros, L., and F. Martínez G., 1988. *Mamíferos silvestres de Honduras.* Tegucigalpa, Honduras: Asociación Hondureña de Ecología. 129 pp.

Melquist, W. E., 1984. *Status Survey of Otters (Lutrinae) and Spotted Cats (Felidae) in Latin America.* Gland, Switzerland: Report to IUCN. 269 pp.

Miller, S. D., and D. D. Everett (eds.), 1986. *Cats of the World: Biology, Conservation and Management.* Washington, D.C.: National Wildlife Federation. 501 pp.

Murie, O. J., 1954. *A Field Guide to Animal Tracks.* Boston: Houghton Mifflin Company. 373 pp.

Noss, R. F., and A. Y. Cooperrider, 1994. *Saving Nature's Legacy, Protecting and Restoring Biodiversity.* Washington, D.C.: Island Press. 416 pp.

Nowak, R. M., 1991. *Walker's Mammals of the World,* 5th ed., vol. 2. Baltimore: Johns Hopkins University Press. 1629 pp.

Nowell, K., P. Jackson, and the IUCN/SSC Cat Specialist Group, 1995. *Wild Cats: Status Survey and Conservation Action Plan.* Cambridge, England: IUCN/SSC Cat Specialist Group. 406 pp.

Olin, G., 1982. *Mammals of the Southwest Desert.* Globe, Ariz.: Southwest Parks and Monuments Association. 99 pp.

Poglyen-Neuwall, I., 1966. Notes on Care, Display and Breeding of Olingos, *Bassaricyon. International Zoological Yearbook* 6: 169–171.

Rabinowitz, A., 1986. *Jaguar: One Man's Struggle to Establish the World's First Jaguar Preserve.* New York: Arbor House Publishing Company. 367 pp.

Reaka-Kudla, M. L., D. E. Wilson, and E. O. Wilson (eds.), 1997. *Biodiversity II: Understanding and Protecting Our Biological Resources.* Washington, D.C.: Joseph Henry Press. 551 pp.

Redford, K. H., and J. G. Robinson, 1991. Park Size and the Conservation of Forest Mammals in Latin America, pp. 227–234. In: M. A. Mares and D. J. Schmidly, 1991. *Latin American Mammalogy: History, Biodiversity, and Conservation.* Norman: University of Oklahoma Press. 468 pp.

Reid, F. A., 1997. *A Field Guide to the Mammals of Central America and Southeast Mexico.* New York and Oxford: Oxford University Press. 334 pp.

Rezendes, P., 1992. *Tracking and the Art of Seeing: How to Read Animal Tracks and Signs.* Charlotte, Vt: Camden House Publishing, Inc. 319 pp.

Robinson, J. G., and K. H. Redford (eds.), 1991. *Neotropical Wildlife Use and Conservation.* Chicago: University of Chicago Press. 520 pp.

Schemmitz, S. D., 1980. *Wildlife Management Techniques Manual.* Washington, D.C.: Wildlife Society. 686 pp.

Schreiber, A., R. Wirth, M. Riffel, H. van Rompaey, and the IUCN/SSC Mustelid and Viverrid Specialist Group, 1989. *Weasels, Civets, Mongooses and Their Relatives: An Action Plan for the Conservation of Mustelids and Viverrids.* London: IUCN/SSC Mustelid and Viverrid Specialist Group. 99 pp.

Sleeper, B., 1995. *Wildcats of the World.* New York: Crown Publishers. 216 pp.

Soulé, M. E., 1987. *Viable Populations for Conservation.* Cambridge: Cambridge University Press. 189 pp.

Stokes, D., and L. Stokes, 1986. *A Guide to Animal Tracking and Behavior.* Boston and Toronto: Little, Brown and Company. 418 pp.

Tello, J., 1979. *Mamíferos de Venezuela.* Caracas, Venezuela: Fundación La Salle de Ciencias Naturales. 192 pp.

Timm, R. M., D. E. Wilson, B. L. Clauson, R. K. LaVal, and C. S. Vaughan, 1989. *Mammals of the La Selva-Braulio Carrillo Complex, Costa Rica.*

Washington, D.C.: United States Department of the Interior Fish and Wildlife Service. 162 pp.

Turner, A., and M. Antón, 1997. *The Big Cats and Their Fossil Relatives: An Illustrated Guide to Their Evolution and Natural History.* New York: Columbia University Press. 234 pp.

Vaughan, C., 1983. *A Report on Dense Forest Habitat for Endangered Wildlife Species in Costa Rica.* Mimeograph. Heredia, Costa Rica: National University. 99 pp.

Weidemann, K., 1987. *Fauna de Venezuela.* Caracas, Venezuela: Oscar Todtmann Editores. 160 pp.

Werdelin, L., 1985. Small Pleistocene Felines of North America. *Journal of Vertebrate Paleontology* 5: 194–210.

Whitaker, J. O., Jr., 1996. *National Audubon Society Field Guide to North American Mammals,* 2nd ed. New York: Chanticleer Press, Inc. 938 pp.

Widholzer, F. L., M. Bergmann, and C. Zotz, 1981. Breeding the Little Spotted Cat. *International Zoo News* 28: 17–22.

Wozencraft, W. C., 1995. "Order Carnivora," electronic version. In: D. E. Wilson and D. M. Reeder (eds.), 1993. *Mammal Species of the World: A Taxonomic and Geographic Reference,* 2nd ed. Washington and London: Smithsonian Institution Press. 1207 pp.

INDEX

illustrations, 193, 195, 197, 198, 199, 200; measurements, 196; origin of name, 196; reproduction, 198–200; taxonomy and relatives, 195–196. *See also Urocyon: U. cinereoargenteus*

Green Arrow, 224

Greytown (Nicaragua), 172. *See also* San Juan del Norte

Grison, 9, 125, 126, 131, 157–162, 166; behavior, 160–162; common names, 158–159; conservation status, 162; dental formula, 159; description, 159; distribution map, 161; habitat and distribution, 160; illustrations, 157, 159, 160, 161, 162; measurements, 159; reproduction, 162; taxonomy and relatives, 158. *See also Galictis: G. vittata*

Guácimo. *See Guazuma*

Guanacaste (Costa Rica), 21, 187, 189

Guanacaste Conservation Area, 6

Guanacaste National Park, 21, 34, 136, 184, 189

Guatemala, 4, 8, 21, 52, 68, 118

Guatuso (Costa Rica), 172

Guazuma, 7

Gulo, 131. *See also Eira barbara*

Guyana, 209

Habitat fragmentation, 32, 221

Hagnauer, Lilly and Werner, 59

Heliconia Biological Field Station (Costa Rica), 151

Herpailurus, 24, 54, 68; *H. yaguarondi*, 24, 65, 67, 131, 223, 229; *H. yagouaroundi (yaguaroundi)*, 68

Herpestidae, 9

Hog-nosed skunk, 139, 145, 146, 150–156; behavior, 154–155; common names, 153; conservation status, 155; dental formula, 153–154; description, 153; distribution map, 155; habitat and distribution, 154; illustrations, 150, 152, 154, 156; measurements, 153; reproduction, 155; taxonomy and relatives, 152–153. *See also Conepatus: C. semistriatus*

Honduras, 8, 21, 36, 52, 68, 103, 109, 118, 136, 153, 196, 224

Hooded skunk, 136–144, 146, 153; behavior, 140–143; common names, 139;

conservation status, 144; dental formula, 140; description, 139–140; distribution map, 141; habitat and distribution, 140; illustrations, 137, 139, 141, 142, 143, 145; kittens, 143–144; measurements, 140; n-Butyl Mercaptan, 140, 143; reproduction, 143–144; smell, ways to eliminate, 143; spraying, 140; taxonomy and relatives, 139. *See also Mephitis: M. macroura*

Hura, 7

Hurricane Caesar, 67, 128

Hyaenidae, 9

Hymenaea, 7

Hyparrhenia rufa, 184. *See also* jaragua

Iguana, 30

Inbreeding, 217–218

Indio-Maíz Biological Reserve (Nicaragua), 111, 218

International Union for the Conservation of Nature. *See* IUCN

IUCN, 210, 214, 220, 223; Red List, 210

Jackal, 9

Jaguar, 2, 14, 19, 21–32, 36, 221; attacks on humans, 32; behavior, 27–30; black, melanistic, 25; caller, 29; common names, 24; conservation status, 32; cubs, 31–32; dental formula, 26; description, 24–26; distribution map, 29; habitat and distribution, 26–27; illustrations, 22, 26, 27, 28, 30, 31; longevity, 32; measurements, 25–26; reproduction, 30–32; taxonomy and relatives, 24; territories, 29–30; threats, 32. *See also Panthera: P. onca*

Jaguarundi, 21, 24, 41, 65–73, 108, 131, 229; aggressive behavior, 70–71; behavior, 70–71; color phases, 68; common names, 68; conservation status, 73; dental formula, 69; description, 68–69; distribution map, 71; habitat and distribution, 69; home range, 71; illustrations, 66, 68–69, 70, 72, 73; kittens, 73; measurements, 68–69; reproduction, 71–73; taxonomy and relatives, 67–68; threats, 73; vocalizations, 71. *See also Herpailurus: H. yaguarondi*

Janzen, Daniel, 215, 225
Jaragua, 34, 184
Jentinkia, 118. *See also Bassariscus*
Jiménez, Marvin, 157–158

Kennett Square, Pennsylvania, 194
Kinkajou, 77–78, 100–109, 111, 112–114, 116–119; behavior, 106–108; common names, 103–104; conservation status, 109; dental formula, 104; description, 104; distribution map, 107; habitat and distribution, 104–106; illustrations, 101, 102, 106, 107, 108; measurements, 104; natural enemies, 108; prehensile tail, 104; reproduction, 109; taxonomy and relatives, 103; vocalizations, 108; young, 109. *See also Potos flavus*

Lake Nicaragua, 172
Las Flores, 100, 164
Las Pumas, 59
Leopardus, 24, 44, 52, 60, 68; *L. pardalis*, 24, 41, 44, 52, 60, 223; *L. tigrina*, 59; *L. tigrinus*, 24, 44, 45, 52, 223, 229; *L. wiedii*, 24, 44, 50, 60, 223, 227. *See also* margay; ocelot; tiger cat
Leopold, A. Starker, 194
Leptospires, 190
Lesser Artilles, 93
Long-tailed weasel, 13, 131, 163–170; behavior, 167–169; common names, 166; conservation status, 169; delayed implantation, 169; dental formula, 167; description, 166–167; distribution map, 169; habitat and distribution, 167; hunting, 167; illustrations, 163, 166–167, 168, 169, 170; measurements, 167; reproduction, 169; skull illustration, 168; taxonomy and relatives, 166; young, 169. *See also Mustela: M. frenata*
Lontra, 173; *L. canadensis*, 173, 177; *L. felina*, 174; *L. longicaudis*, 11, 131, 174, 175, 223; *L. provocax*, 174. *See also* marine otter; Neotropical river otter; Northern river otter; Southern river otter
Los Chiles (Costa Rica), 172
Louisville Zoo, 110

Lutra. See Lontra
Lutrinae, 174

Magpie jay, 90
Maíz River (Nicaragua), 111
Manatees, 111
Mangrove forest, 7, 99, 219
Manilkara, 7, 189; *M. zapota*, 11
Marenco Biological Field Station (Costa Rica), 207
Margay, 44. *See Leopardus: L. wiedii*
Margay, 21, 24, 41, 44, 50–58, 60, 61, 65, 68, 108, 128, 227; ankle joint, rotating, 53, 55, 227; behavior, 54–55; common names, 52; conservation status, 58; dental formula, 54; description, 52–53; distribution map, 55; habitat and distribution, 54; illustrations, 50, 52, 53, 54, 56, 57, 58; measurements, 52–53; reproduction, 57; taxonomy and relatives, 51–52; territories, 55; threats, 58; young, 57. *See also Leopardus: L. wiedii*
Marine otter, 174. *See also Lontra: L. felina*
Maritza Biological Field Station (Costa Rica), 21, 65, 184
Martes, 126
Mazama americana, 38
Meganteron, 4
Mephitinae, 166
Mephitis, 131, 152; *M. macroura*, 136, 139, 141, 145, 146, 153; *M. mephitis*, 139, 140. *See also* American striped skunk; hooded skunk
Mexico, 4, 27, 36, 45, 52, 77, 82, 84, 93, 104, 118, 120, 121, 131, 139, 154, 159, 160, 166, 174, 185, 187
Miacidae, 3
Montane forest, 8, 219, 228
Morpho, 90
Mustela, 131, 159, 166; *M. frenata*, 13, 131, 163, 166, 167, 168. *See also Eira barbara*; long-tailed weasel
Mustelidae, 9, 123–178, 174, 223, 224; breeding, 126; delayed implantation in, 126; hunting, 125; musk gland, 125; pelt trade, 126
Mustelinae, 166

Pteronura brasiliensis, 173

Puma, 2, 11, 14, 21, 24, 27, 33–41, 68, 90; attacks on humans, 41; behavior, 38; common names, 36; conservation status, 41; cubs, 40–41; dental formula, 36; description, 36; distribution map, 40; habitat and distribution, 37; illustrations, 33, 35, 37, 38, 39; measurements, 36; melanistic, 36; reproduction, 40; taxonomy and relatives, 35; territories, 40. *See also Puma*

Puma, 35; *P. concolor*, 11, 24, 33, 35, 90; *P.c.coryi*, 218; *P.c. costaricencis*, 36, 223; *P.c. cougar*, 35, 37, 223; *P.c. mayensis*, 36. *See also* puma

Quercus, 8

Rabinowitz, Alan, 29

Raccoon, 9, 11, 15, 40, 77–78, 82, 89–100, 103, 118, 188; behavior, 96–99; as carriers of disease, 100; common names, 93; conservation status, 99–100; dental formula, 94; description, 93; distribution map, 96; food washing, 92, 97–99; habitat and distribution, 94–96; illustrations, 92, 93, 95, 97, 98, 99; measurements, 93–94; pelt and pelt trade, 99–100; reproduction, 99; taxonomy and relatives, 92–93; young, 99. *See also Procyon*

Rain forest, 7, 26, 37, 47, 54, 69, 84, 114, 202, 219, 228

Red fox, 13, 192

Rhea, 209

Riba, Pablo, 207

Ring-tailed cat, 77–78, 117–122; behavior, 120–121; common names, 118; conservation status, 121–122; dental formula, 118; description, 118; distribution map, 120; habitat and distribution, 120; illustrations, 117, 118, 119, 121, 122; reproduction, 121; taxonomy and relatives, 118. *See also Bassariscus: B. astutus*

Ritualized behavior, 21; in cats, 21; in canids, 181–182

River otter, 9, 11, 68, 125, 126, 131; behavior, 176–177; common names, 174; conservation status, 178; dental formula, 174; description, 174; distribution map, 175; habitat and distribution, 174–176; illustrations, 171, 173, 175, 176, 177; measurements, 174; reproduction, 177–178; taxonomy and relatives, 173–174; tool use, 176; vocalizations, 176; young, 176. *See also Lontra: L. longicaudis*

Saber-toothed cats, 4, 25, 228

San Juan del Norte (Nicaragua), 111

San Juan River Basin, 111, 172

Santa Rosa National Park (Costa Rica), 11–12, 23, 28, 34, 90, 144, 221

San Vito Biological Station (Costa Rica), 207

Sarapiquí (Costa Rica), 172

Sea otter. *See Enhydra lutris*

Shoemaker's tree. *See Byrsonima crassifolia*

Short-eared dog, 182. *See also* small-eared dog

Skunk, 9, 11, 125, 126, 131; smell, 16, 158, 166

Sloth, 30

Small-eared dog, 185, 201–205; behavior, 205; common names, 204; conservation status, 205; dental formula, 204; description, 204; distribution map, 205; habitat and distribution, 204; illustrations, 201, 203; measurements, 204; reproduction, 205; taxonomy and relatives, 204. *See also Atelocynus: A. microtis*

Smilodon, 4

Southern river otter, 173–174. *See also Lontra: L. provocax*

Species, number of, 216

Speothus, 207; *S. venaticus*, 185, 205, 207, 209, 223, 229. *See also* bush dog

Spider monkey. *See Ateles geoffroyi*

Spilogale, 131, 145, 152; *S. putorius*, 138, 139, 144, 145, 147, 153. *See also* spotted skunk

Spotted skunk, 138, 139, 144–149, 152, 153; behavior, 147; common names, 146; conservation status, 149; dental formula, 147; description, 146–147; distribution map, 149; habitat and distribution, 147; handstand position,